INHERITANCE
TAX

Poems 1998-2008

INHERITANCE TAX

JASON FLOYD WILLIAMS

INTERIOR NOISE PRESS
Austin, TX

INHERITANCE TAX
Copyright © 2008 by Jason Floyd Williams

For order information and current mailing address please visit www.interiornoisepress.com

Interior Noise Press
P.O. Box 17084
Austin, TX 78760

The author gratefully acknowledges the following publications where some of these poems first appeared: *My Favorite Bullet, City Poetry,* and *Nerve Cowboy.*

Cover Photograph by Laura Williams

Library of Congress Control Number: 2008925585

ISBN 978-0-9816606-0-8

First Edition

for Trinity

Contents

'My son,' the father said, 'you are always with me, and everything I have is yours. But we had to celebrate and be glad, because this brother of yours was dead and is alive again; he was lost and is found.'

—Luke 15:31

Nothin' feels better than blood on blood.

—Bruce Springsteen
"Highway Patrolman"

the pull of destiny.

After performing
a small surgery
on a dying roof,
my grandfather and I
went to a strip joint.

Unknown to us
that we would meet
Destiny,
and that she
would do
a lap
dance for us.

my life before you.

I was pretty drunk on Jim Beam &
she was very high on skunk weed &
we were watching the snowflakes cover up
her little porch like an ADHD student's
still life photography project.

The ragged couch was near the
glass doors & her porch lights
reflected each snowflake.
It was peaceful, I remember that.

I also remember Bill was supposed
to call us around 8pm & it
was 9:30.
My mind began to demolition-derby
all sorts of thoughts.
For instance, Bill had died when his
Chevy S-10 skidded off Myers Road
& crashed into Lake Erie—through
the snow & ice—& there he remained
like the forgotten banana popsicle
in the back of the freezer.
The family needed to divvy-up Bill's kids.
Julie, the oldest, went to his widow
& her family.
Willie, the youngest, went w/ Bill's folks.
And me & Heather, through some
big hole in Children's Services, got Vicki,
the middle kid.
Heather quit dancing at Cinderella's
& got a job waitressing at Lou's Diner.
I dropped out of school & started
roofing at the family business.

We were doin' alright—
Vicki liked the cats & spiral staircase

at Heather's place &
we even went to PTA meetings.

Vicki was in the 4th grade when
Bill called & said he had to
work late tonight.

I was a little disappointed
to hear from him.

miss teen america contest.

After hearing
Miss Teen Idaho
explain her desires
to domesticate
a cougar,
I put down
my hand lotion
and turned off
the TV.

shared loneliness.

Paramecium & flagellum shapes argue over
bar counter space w/ cigarette burns
& junior high swastikas;
I just stare until
the hillbilly stripper—in the drop
of conversation with some ol'
troll bastard (I'd respect 'im
more if he said: "Ya know,
why don't we fuck?" instead of
this long road of psychology:
"So, tell me 'bout yer parents...")
—invites me to the stage.
She proves the joint doesn't
give dental insurance when
she smiles.
It's group therapy & she's
not dancing.
I take off.
Benny Goodman throbbin' loud
in my ears as I pass a
recently gutted development lot.
In the exact middle is one
young tall tree—the lone soccer player
that survived the plane crash
into the Alps.
At first, I yell: "Grow, tree, grow!"
Then, as I curve past a cemetery,
an apartment complex, it begins
to irritate me.
That tree is the elephant boy;
a nosey colonist staked at
the edge of hostile Indian territory;
that tree is alone.

Benny's still transfusin' my blood
when I borrow my grandfather's

axe & flannel shirt, drive back,
walk 300 yards, apologize
to the tree, then cut it down.

truck stop romances.

I started off pumpin' diesel
for 18-wheelers & eventually
was promoted to gasoline.

I was 2nd shift, 4pm to midnight &
busted my tail pumpin' gas
into cars & mainly tourist RV's—
these well-off retirees that
would buy $30,000 campers to escape
from suburbia & park next to
others in the same boat.
They'd form "camping communities"
where everyone would elect Mayors
& Secretaries & Councils & Sheriffs.
Playin' House. Playin' Politics.
All the wives looked like
stuffed turkies & the hubbies
were animated skeletons.

Ah, well, it wasn't such
a terrible gig.

There was Red—
He was about 10 yrs older
than me & drove a
furniture truck.
He had the hots for my mother
& would bug her at the bar
she worked at.

He was slightly nuts, but would
slip me some good joints, like
a lobbyist w/ the hopes I'd
put in a decent word
w/ my mom.

The spring evenings were crisp
like fresh celery, & the diesel & gasoline
fumes that swirled around us
were concealed by night, like a Van Gogh
painting underwater.
Occasionally, I'd get some all right tips.
Like the time two girls, around my age,
gave me $10 in ones & waited
around for me to
count 'em.

Maybe they wanted a date or
a phone number or a male participant
in their sex orgy—
I never added it up.

I wasn't quite myself.
I had just gotten out of
the psych-ward & was prescribing
myself dope & LSD
to help my anxieties.

career choices.

"Perhaps some of us have to go through dark and devious ways before we can find the river of Peace or the high road to the soul's destination." Dreams and Personality

for my father.

Part 1.
There were truckloads.
Sanford & Son old Ford pick-up
truckloads of broken, brown
beer glass—
the kids waitin' for the bus
might have thought he
was delivering shale rock
to the history museum.

Towards the end,
he had 46 Miller Lites sharin'
his day—
each one a comforting blurb,
a separate toast to a
separate cause.
2 cases sittin' shotgun
like a chubby toddler, his
arm tenderly 'round them;
teenage son ridin' lonesome
in the back seat.

He took the boy out
a few times—
mainly to a dive bar called
Flamingos, where
father & son would sit w/
ragged others like
awkward musical notes along
the bar counter.

Picture all those cowboy bars
that Eastwood would walk
into & gather 20
dirty looks, or *Star Wars'*
Mos Eisley cantina w/out
the rogue aliens.
Yeah, like that.
All the Hell's Angels had
menstrual blood under their
fingernails &
someone else's flesh
on their skull rings.

And dancers, and dancers.
The dancers were flies.
They were bent on
bikers & drugs,
not just blood &
implantation of eggs.

The truckloads of glass kept
coming out of this hidden driveway,
as if it were a union construction site
or a recently established
frat house.

A busy ant, this guy.

Part 2.
What changed everything was
when his '75 Cadillac boat
Chubby Checkered a 180—hopin'
to upstage Camus—sped 60+mph,
backwards,
towards an innocent family,

a church family,
that had to swerve to
avoid a night collision w/
2 Red Demon Eyes.

Part 3.
His wife was gone.
His kids, too.
The Caddie destroyed.
The dancers found others.
The woman that busted up
the marriage wasn't there.

He got the house back, though.

And it was full of fleas.

Part 4.
A dozen. A hundred.
A hundred dozen fleas
everywhere.
They were left by his
ex's dogs, a couple of
German Sheperds that
behaved like poor losers
from the Big Pedigree Show after
the divorce: attacking
each other; shitting on everything;
chewing off their
flea collars.

Part 5.
This Rasputin lost in Northeastern
Ohio's biker community, now here—
on this geometric slate floor—fish-flopping

in front of a 10-inch black & white TV tossin'
static snowstorm silhouettes onto
this circus contortion of a man, this
helpless newborn mole in an
underground home, a human
being pilfered for real estate
where fleas can raise
their families;
build their malls.

Part 6.
He detoxed himself.
A 2-decade career sweated out
over a week of
nightmares involving
disembowelment, snakes, fleas.
When he was ready
to give up, he asked
Christ for help.
Just to sleep w/out
the nightmares.
Caravaggio should've painted
this Conversion.

Part 7.
13 sober years later—
he tells me about
a recent A.A. lead he heard
w/ some fella who
trashed his vehicle
in a Convenient Mart
parking lot to
avoid hitting a
pink elephant crossing
the road.

early deaths.

*"Death, that strange being with the square toes who
lived way in the West." Zora Neale Hurston*

My friend told me recently
that all the schools around
here Photoshop out the
rolled eyes, stuck out tongues,
messy hair, & obscene gestures
from the class photos.

There aren't any more class clowns.
It's all artificial now.
Almost like Disney World.

My 1st grade class pictures were
an early success in burn-out
tracking.
Nearly all the kids w/
dirty wrinkled shirts &
mini-beehive-blendered-haircuts
became hoodlums.
Heather may have become
a majorette, but she
twirled that baton between drags
of Kools; Scott may have
become a good running back,
but he smuggled swigs of Pabst
during practice.

Then there was Louie—
a tiny dustbin remnant of
a boy who showed me my
1st picture of a naked lady.
She was the 8 of Diamonds, I think,
w/ black hair & big boobs, showing
all her stuff for all the curious

little kids & lonely truckers
around the states.

Louie's brother, Rick, was a year
or 2 older than me—
we used to watch kids fall
off the monkey bars to the
cracked concrete below
during recess.

Louie & Rick never got the
chances to cop feels w/ girls,
to drink beer behind school,
or to get high before gym class.
You see, during that summer,
Louie & Rick went out in a small
boat, w/ 2 men & a dog,
onto Lake Erie.
The boat capsized during
a storm & only the dog
came back.
A beagle, I think.

Some girl—a girl who always
reminded me of Miss Piggy—
told me their bodies
washed up on her beach.

I don't know about that.

But I know they died.
My mother showed me
the newspaper article
& asked me if I knew them.

"Yeh. They're my friends."

less than 12 items.

As she pulled her daughter
closer to her 12-lbs of Saran-wrapped
ground beef, & further
from my 6-lbs of grapefruit,
I told her:
"Ya know, I've never kidnapped
anyone before. Let alone a kid.
Wait—that isn't entirely true.
There was Angela.
She told me her parents were
cruel, almost tyrants.
Bill & I picked her up after
school. She ended up
staying in my car for 8 hrs
while we assembled vacuum cleaner parts
in a square factory.
She was going to live in Bill's trailer,
behind his parents' place.
Our stray.
But the cops were after us.
She left us to call her parents.
The moon reflected her eyes.
Eyes like a young Lauren Bacall,
eyes that punch the sternum
& allow chunks of bones to float,
not pay highway tolls,
throughout the blood."
She paid for her groceries
in quick-draw, exact-change check.
Pushed the stuffed cart, kid in front,
quickly outside.
The cashier didn't even
ask how I was.

excessive drinking.

I had made an agreement
w/ myself, a couple weeks back,
to only drink booze
on special occasions.

So we were on our way
to the dog show & I already
had 7 beers in me &
had grand promises
of more to come.

It was a weird scene,
the dog show, that is.
All the dog owners—w/ their
decorative sweaters &
curtain-length dresses—had
strange ostrich gaits
& seemed to be terribly exhausted
after their little marches
around the child-safe
fence.

All the dogs were done up
like supermodels,
except one.

This lone dog, & I don't know how
this ugly footstool got in—maybe its
owner had connections—but this thing
was a gruesome, turd-brown pug
w/ severe asthma—like those lizards from
Land of the Lost—& it had all sorts of
moldy green gunk around those bug eyes.
Oh, yeah—it was fat.
Circus tent fat.

In fact, the owner had to pull
the thing out on a
beat up red wagon.

I was the only one that cheered
for that miserable mutt—
that creature hidden in the
basement when company came over.

And later, when I drank
4 more beers—& they awarded
the Best in Show ribbon to
some stuck-up cocker spaniel
w/ pink ribbons on its ears, braids
on its plush hair, & neatly
painted toenails—
I was ripe w/ anger &
I hopped the gate & bit
that gorgeous sonabitch
right in the head.

I don't know much after that,
I guess I blacked out.

But when I'm outta jail, if
that cocker spaniel survives
the operations, I'm going
to buy that damn pug.

by the eggs, aisle 12.

I tried not to
run her over, and
succeeded.

Then inside
the grocery store,
she saw me
carrying a bottle
of whiskey, and
I saw her
carrying a container
of milk, and
we knew it
would fail.

silverfish travel.

in pairs—like good away teams
should—out of a naked
electrical outlet,
only to be dowsed w/ Windex,
by me.

Tomorrow, another couple will come
looking for their lost relatives, missing
friends.

I stare at myself
in the bathroom mirror

and think about marriage.

surrogate muses.

Part 1.
When I wake, my mind
wombles back to yesterday—
Tom doin' Heston from *Apes*,
chest jutted out, arms
splayed sideways, yelling:
"It's a madhouse! Madhouse!"
while I jumped crazed-gorilla,
imaginary hose in hands.
Later, we all journeyed
into a thick jock forest.
Bob brought an inflatable
Spider-man & thunked fast
several big men who
must live w/barbers &
threaten them daily
for trims.
When they got angry,
he simply said: "It's the super-hero,
not me."
The ventriloquist alibi.

Tonight, we're able
to sing/screech karaoke again.
New bar: The Eagles.

2 seats over, at our
shared round table,
is Ernie.
Ernie's a 79-yr-old Iwo Jima vet.
He stands & does
wild, wind-up convulsions
on the dance floor.

I buy him a couple drafts,
thank 'im for my freedom &

we yell together when Bill
belts out a Johnny tune.
Further into the night,
forgotten amounts of booze—
at least a couple White Russians
in me—we're at a strip joint.

I give the gal in
the mermaid dress—
someone abducted from my
subconscious puddles—
a John Adams statue, 2 plastic piglets
& a rubber snake because
I'm broke.
She's thrilled & gives
me a hug—
shows me her Polaroid
in the stripper-family album.
Her name, Leslie, is
kinda hot-stamped to her
upper arm.
Almost charcoaled.
I notice it while we're standing
outside watching a lesbian dancer
duel w/her sister
in the snow.
We're all angels w/ dirty faces
wrestling w/someone,
I think.

Part 2.
I had lost my muse
2 wks earlier.
K—for whom every poem I've
written is meant to seduce,
to woo—

told this F fella—an ugly avocado
student of early cummings trash,
a 50+ man that lies in his poetry—
that he was a genius.
He sat up quickly
(the positive test subject
a pioneering Viagra might've needed)
smirking.
Since then, things have
been
disjointed.

I ask Leslie out for coffee
when the girls are done fighting.

siblings.

When Lindsay was unable to pick
the fridge's padlock,
she'd loot the cupboards—
snaggin' 2-lb bags of flour,
a couple old tortilla shells,
& some stale saltines—
then scurry back
to her bedroom, like a
gambling junkie w/ a pile
of scratch-offs.

I was drivin' to Dairy Mart
for booze, havin'
PCP hallucinations 'bout a
young cheerleader joggin' against
my car at 45 mph, then
cuttin' me off &
sneakin' into her house.

When I got home,
I called the girl's mother
to complain.

shooting a dog.

Part 1.
Merle's dogs—one bloodhound, w/ real
saggy eyes & an Orson Welles from
The Trial tiredness to it, & one
husky-wolf mix w/ savage *Texas Chainsaw*
killing eyes—came over into our yard
while Lindsay & me were swingin' on
the playset & immediately started
growlin' at us like we were the ones
that fed 'em dry dog food instead
of Alpo & gravy.

We were cornered & they kept crawlin'
towards us—all hunched over, like
the preliminary werewolf stage—
& all we could do was yell for help!

Our mom saw the dogs' thought-bubbles
w/ meaty kids for dessert & she got
our ol man who, in turn, got his
shotgun in fast Alamo style.

He fired one warning shot above the
dogs' heads & this sent the ol' bloodhound
headin' home—its heart just wasn't in it;
it only wanted the shits & giggles
of scarin' kids.
But the husky-wolf was an
authentic mean & it
continued to come.
So my dad put a blast of bullets
to its chest—& as if
out of pure spite—
that sucker got back up
like Dracula w/ an aluminum foil
stake in his heart.

So my ol man re-loaded & got 'im again.
That was that. We poked it w/
some sticks as my dad put his gun
away & went to tell Merle.

Part 2.
Merle, our neighbor, had served a couple
tours in Korea & had the severed
ears to prove it—a dozen or so—
my friend Bill told me.
3 or 4 each shoved fraternity-phone-booth
tight into old mayo jars.

Bill's dad & Merle were pals from
the Army, so the kids were expected
to see that kinda stuff.
Young Bill told me of awkward times when
he & his kid sister would sit on
Merle's bed, eatin' old rock candy, starin'
at various dusty medals, ribbons,
& the ears, near the window,
like they needed sunlight.

Later in life, Merle's wife would get
Alzheimer's bad & almost wander into
my dad's pot plants, hidden in the garden
between the corn & tomatoes.
When she died, Merle married his
step-daughter; some "Miss Carny
of Somewhere" & occasional fill-in
for the Fabulous Fat Lady.

But that was years after Bill's dad
talked Merle outta shootin' us—
me & my sister— to get even
for his dog.

Every day that summer he watched
us, 70 yards from his house, swingin'
on the big oak tree—
our tree of life.

Part 3.
Old Bill acted as a sorta diplomat between
my dad & Merle. He arranged for them
to meet each other,
over the ragged red fence
my father had put up between the properties,
& there they shook w/their left hands.

Their right hands held tight to
the pistols in their pockets.

prodigal sons.

So he followed his ol man
to Toldeo w/ the gold miner's
gusto that believes in
radio DJs that proclaim
on Monday
the number of days
until the weekend.
It was the living in
between that he never
got the hang of.

So the father ruined
his liver, housed w/ his
landladies, & was
eventually UPSed back to
Geneva in a pine box
wearing a Salvation Army suit.

The son screwed around &
caught AIDS.

In the progression of time—
those days in the middle—
he lost his gas station job &
Ford Escort.

He, too, came back to Geneva.
But by train, & wearing
Goodwill safari gear.

His mother wasn't much better off:
her trailer's ceiling hung like
a tall cow's udder & the feral cats
formed agreements w/ the
domesticated ones
that resulted in a constant

fur-flurry wherever
you stepped.

He moved in there.
Occupied a space 12-by-12,
& debated w/ Welfare
for a monthly block
of cheese.

There's more to it,
of course.

Like his father & my grandfather,
dirty twins growing up filthy poor—
potato soup-for-every-meal poor—
in Hick, PA &
counterfeiting their ol man's
handwriting, at age 6, to get
tabbed beer
& cigarettes.

Later, they would roll down a
steep hill, drunk, w/ their
pal named Rabbit.

remedial english.

The 3rd pair of boobs I saw
were in my 9th grade
English class.
Mr. Lucas—a failed bar bouncer,
a worn out backup for
Andy Capp on his hangover days—
was showing us *Conan the Barbarian*:
the uncensored version.

When the scene w/ the breasts
came on—some warrior chick's tits,
or slave girl's jugs, or crazy
witch's teets, I forget
which—Mr. Lucas used this
opportunity, while all the boys
were superglued to the TV,
to pressure Susie Reed
into doing extra credit.

I saw it cause Mary Ann Lopez
pointed it out to me.

It made me feel awkward,
I remember, watching
this fleshy-red Michelin Man
pushing poor Susie into
the corner.

Mr. Lucas propped his arms
against the walls as if they were
sliding rulers to fence her in.

Susie used a lot of creativity
to get out of that situation.

a couple good ones.

Dogs will hump each other's heads
to show dominance; cowardly hooligans
will dive-bomb ya when your
back is turned—

and while waitin' 45 minutes
for the cops to arrive after a mid-80's
Buick plows into my friend's
stopped car; a young thug
haulin' near 50mph when he hits us
& close to it when
I race 2 blocks after 'im,
then stand fixed, neck-tight—
a tough customer for the guillotine;
eyes stocked in Klingon madness
& getting more mad each minute as
citizens drive by
laughingcursinggigglinghollering at
our smashed vehicle—I yell like
Cagney would've if he'd done R flicks:
"Shaddup, ya fuckers! Fuck all of ya!
I'll skull-drag the lottafya!"

A white trash detective in an
unmarked Olds—
Quiet Riot fan mullet, wormish mustache
shimmying towards chin—
asks me, as I'm
still hurling curses at
fools drivin' by, hopin' the sucker
that hit us comes back:
"Did you call me a Motherfucker?"
"If you drove by and called
me names then I did."
"I'll bash yer head into
that fence."

Tomorrow, Sandy the barber will tell me
how he recovered from his stroke,
at the age of 72, in a single week
w/ the help of his son.

I'll nod, as he buzzes
the stateline on my neck,
& watch a uniform parade
of ants carry dead skin & hair
back to their kids.

strain theory.

*"According to strain theory, when juveniles experience
strain or stress, they become upset, and they sometimes engage
in delinquency as a result." Robert Agnew*

Part 1.
Freud said our
second expulsion from Paradise
occurs when we're
weaned from
our mothers.

When I was three—
already upset w/the
weaning bit—my
grandmother Janet came into the
room where I was playing w/some
Mad Max: Beyond Thunderdome idea
in a clothes basket &
emptied all my toys
into pinata puddles on
the floor.

I just remember this
vinegar-baking powder-
volcano diorama eruption
of anger as I scrambled outside, yanked
her pants down, and
took a bite outta
her ass.

My mother and uncle
had to pull
me off.

Part 2.
The Norse Sisters of Fate
arrange for me

to be drunk, 23 yrs later, w/my friends
& complaining about my
co-workers—
one of 'em, this
Dune Sandworm, human-pieces parts,
DNA lot won
on eBay;
this unruly, mad child
of Tor from *Plan 9*—
is plopped on a
dining room chair
across from me.
He gets up, a body
pronounced dead w/
different ideas, and
gargantuans towards me &
gives me the best
bitch-slap I've
ever received.

I pull the matador-bitten-by-the-bull
act & encourage
'im to charge w/multiple
flip-booking of middle fingers.
This is the red dot
on his eye exam. He plows,
like so many big, dumb Marvel Comics
villains & all I gotta do
is sidestep &
watch his chunk of head
bounce off
the couch cushions.

I grasshopper on 'im &
bite his noggin like it's
made outta chocolate.

Bill and Mike have to pull
me off.

The Blob has learned his lesson—
he's one of the flunkies
in the school boiler room—
so he proportions himself
back into the same chair (or
its fraternal twin) &
begins to cry as
streams of blood
yarn into
his eyes.

bad day for beetles.

When my grandfather was
in love, he wanted
to be reincarnated as a
Japanese beetle.
"All they do is fuck & die.
Not bad."
Today, he's plucking 'em off
hollyhock leaves &
tossing 'em into a soup can
of gas.

Earlier, Morgan told me
I was a large container of
variety nuts.
Not just cashew,
but the whole legume family.
All because I said her
mother still has a good shape.

A week before, Morgan & I
had laid in my truck-bed
groping an' grazing beneath
a black velvet sky.
Saw Frank Lloyd Wright's *Falling Waters*,
thought about her, me & St. Croix.
A good time.
Now I'm a nut.

Two Japanese beetles I've
tossed into the can
are climbing onto a tiny leaf
like the unlucky passengers
on a romantic cruise.

I give it a shake.

time again.

He was no Dillinger, that's
for sure—
& his ragtag teenage crew
wasn't the best that a
small town crime circuit
could offer.

Claudia, his ex, drove
the Mustang thru backwoods
capillaries while Ponch
& cronies shot various
dog tranquilizers & euthanasia
syrup into their legs.

She had to testify
against 'im later on.

She didn't snitch, however,
the time before—when
Ponch & a different brood
busted into an amusement park—
nor on the third attempt
when he had skipped the
final Cliff's Notes pages
on building a meth lab.

She wasn't a canary in
that last example cause the
mock-monster lab blew up
w/a dozen raised-eyebrowed
firemen standing sideline.

I was dating Claudia
briefly
between Ponch's tours
in prison.

And once, we were speeding
thru main drags to the vet's
while I held & massaged the chest

of a tiny kitten her daughter, who
was hollering feral-Comanche
in the back seat, had
accidentally drowned.

The small heartbeats in my hands
like a dying alarm clock.

try to remember.

Part of my morning prayers today
included a thank you to God
for being w/ me when
I went to that bum golfer's place—
that piece of trash that screwed
around w/ Bill's wife—& I had
my biggest wrench hidden
in my Army jacket.

I was drinkin' booze—earlier, in
the parking lot—tryin' to
remember his apartment number.

Thank you, Lord, for not
lettin' him come outside
when I was pushin' on his door—
my hand was sealed to that wrench
& my heart was full of hate.

a plea.

Recently, I've become this
3rd-rate version of Bob Mitchum
in *Cape Fear*—
the loud braggart bellowing like a
wild dingo with its rear legs
caught in a bear trap, watching from
the back at a pseudo-industrial
show where the dames
clothespin their nipples.
The people in front of me—
the people I've been throwin' beer
on for an hour—
could be on their first date.
The young woman says to the new beau:
"Simon, that jerk threw
Bud Lite on my fishnets.
Do something."
Simon keeps looking at me,
doin' his best Gregory Peck
grimace; I keep pourin'.
I've been waitin' months
for somebody to do something.

My newest role model, Theodore Roosevelt,
certainly wouldn't approve.

He & I started off the same—
two kids with rotten bouts
of asthma—
but that's it.

By the time he was my age
he'd been elected to Congress,
married, then widowed, then
married again; spent a
couple yrs in the Dakota badlands &

in a few more years he'd become
Police Commissioner of NYC.

I'm two classes away from
my BA; was arrested 5 months ago;
fall in & out of love
w/strippers—
& today am countin' the scrapes
bruises & gashes after a
night of drunken wrestling.
At the end,
Americans vs Russians:
our micro-Cold War.

never mind the romantics.

"Heaven gives its glimpses only to those
not in position to look too close." Robert Frost

They're called thin places—
these spots where Heaven &
Earth almost touch.

We had such a moment at
the zoo when it started
to rain & we sought cover
underneath some weeping willows
next to the flamingo den.

All these pink, Harryhausen-ish
swizzle sticks kept hopscotching thru
the storm as we huddled against
the wet.

If we had been dating longer,
I'd have proposed.

Instead, that happened in
a far less auspicious setting:
with you jack-hammering fingers
on a very resilient pimple
on my neck.

a family moment.

Snow floats fattly
to the white ground—
we sit, eggnog
in hands—
fireplace warming
our feet.
Rubbing alcohol
on the table—
to put the fleas
we find on
near naked dogs
in.

genealogy.

Uncle George's mind might've
been lug-nutted to *Bonanza's*
live album—w/ Lorne Greene
gnip-gnopping,
This land of mine is
the home of the pine, Ponderosa!—
before he was socked in the
head & his body tangled
w/ seaweed
in a Jersey river.

The family's intro to George's
madness was his
West-Virginia-highway-Bible-reading
tour, which was protested
by the cops.

I remember him
sneaking, bzzzing, on some Quixotic trip,
into my grandparents' place
to stash his totems:
like a chipmunk or
the Easter bunny or
the spy from Stratego.

My father tells me
in front of my new girl:
"Along with madness, you also have
alcohol & substance abuse, anger,
depression, & a couple
other things."

"That's a helluva start
for Trin."

"I'm just setting you straight."

"Thanks."

"So," Trinity asks my dad, "is that the garage you used to hang the pot plants in?"

the robbery.

Mrs. G. was the stereotypical
old woman pushin' 80
w/ a rickety grocery cart—
wearing a brittle brown wig that
seemed to collect all sorts of insects
w/ grand pollinatin' ambitions;
large glasses, that if turned
the opposite way, would melt
her eyes like so many ants
under the tyranny
of magnifying lenses;
a ghostly vestigial tail smell
of utility closets &
food pantries that lingered
behind like Pigpen's
dust cloud.

But she had a good wit
for this Mayberry sister town.
And she was kind,
which always goes
a long way.

Her husband, Mr. G., the restaurant's
founder & namesake, had died
a dozen years back.

I was the night dishwasher,
and would usually find myself
bicep-deep in various decomposing
foods, unclogging the drains—
I complain now, but it was still
better than the pigeon-shit vats
that those sorry
Moroccan tanners would jitterbug
animal hides in.

I would smoke Winstons
at the counter, waiting
for Mrs. G. to finish
counting the day's cash
& receipts.

She used to not have anyone
stay w/ her—
until the robbery, that is.
One of the night cooks
was suspected—Justin,
not Adam.

Adam was in his late 30s, hair like a
deforestation project, & a belly like a kangaroo
rentin' out her pouch to circus clowns.
He was a sad classic rocker
who lived w/ his mom &
sold me leaves & stems
as "good dimebags."

He was a loser, but not
a mean-spirited thief.

Justin, however, was a stir crazy hound—
an average cook
that was always practicing the
"don't-take-your-eyes-off-the-pen" test.
A little man w/ El Gigante aims.
He was as useful
as a redundant colon.

The story goes that Mrs. G. was
gettin' ready to leave the restaurant
around 11pm, her purse fat
with the day's monetary droppings.

As she was closin' the main
back door, 2 guys tried
jaws-of-life-ing her out by
her purse.
Instinctively, or maybe because
of momentum, she fell backwards
into the steel door she hadn't
yet locked & kicked it
closed w/ her feet.
Even though she was pretty shaken
& very bruised up, she managed
to call the cops & give an
accurate description of
one of the guys.
The other one was masked.

Despite the Mayberry similarities,
the small town law reacted quickly &
they caught the unmasked thief
on someone's porch within
an hour.

He just wanted to use the phone,
he said.
The startled homeowners would let him
use it after they made a call of their own—
to the cops.

As the patrol cars pulled closer,
their lights splattering
anti-disco fever against the
American Gothic postcard, they
caught the robber w/ his hands raised high
& shit runnin' down
his pants.
A new Pilates move.

I don't know if the captured thief
coughed-up Justin's name &
Justin had concocted an artificial
alibi, or if the mugger
remained loyal.
All I know is Justin continued
to work for a few weeks—
eyes always dartin', chokin' on
each breath of air he chewed—
until they fired him for
being late.

I didn't mind waiting
for Mrs. G.

The Winstons tasted good
after a tough night of dishwashing.
And every once in a while Adam
would share some good weed—

which lasted most of
the night.

near eden.

The kids stampedin' thru
the livin' room,
haphazardly hopscotchin'
over a sleepin' Lab,
are the kinda kids who'll
cut your hair at 3am &
flood the kitchen when
ya answer the phone.
But now they're fine—
& they help the local newlyweds
I'm lookin' at in the newspaper
strangle their team contentment,
their straight teeth,
their lack of scars,
into my days.
I've been buyin' Johnny West figures
for the past couple weeks.
Buildin' 'em a Lincoln Log cabin,
givin' 'em rifles, fryin' pans,
buffalo blankets, lanterns—
a regular homestead.
I imagine the elder West
sittin' in a rocking chair, hound dog
at his feet, a fireplace glow sharpenin'
his features & helpin' to set the mood
for whatever story or poem he's recitin'
to the kids.
Outside the cabin are monsters:
Frankenstein's abomination
lookin' for orchids,
The Fly collectin' rent,
Blackbeard showin' off a
chest tattoo, The Blob that bugged
McQueen, & various cowboy outlaws
hired thru the local paper,
all waitin' to ransack the family

in one way or another.
There's a great scene in
The Time of Your Life where
James Cagney's character, some classy
drunk, talks to his almost-wife about
their almost-children:
"That third one, he was different.
Dumb & goofy lookin'.
I liked him a lot."
It's that kind of lamentin' over
Frost's *Road Not Taken* that's
been tailin' me for years.
The missed wives, kids.
It was the feeder-fish
in my cerebellum while
I was diggin' thru
some Fantastic Four comics
at Ray's shop.
Then Darlene walked in.
She worked for the post office
& we had bartered glances
a few Saturdays back.
Darlene was in shape from
all that walkin' &
moderately attractive:
straight brown hair, little make-up.
Could probably cook damn
good stuffed peppers.
Maybe even shoot a gun.
One of the closest gals I've
found to Mrs. West.
She cleaved into Ray's & my
sporadic chat about fist fights
to ask me a couple questions:
"So, where are you from?"
"Cleveland."

"Oh, yeah? We're going to a pub
on the west side. *Patrick's*.
You should come."
I wanted to accept, but I couldn't see
if she had a ring on her finger—
damn gloves!
"I'm kinda stuck out here tonight."
"Too bad. So long."
When she left, Ray told me
she was married to a fireman.
"Why did she ask me out?"
"Maybe to cause problems."
When my grandfather used to pick
me up from high school, he'd
honk his horn at the ugly girls.
I'd ask him, after I'd peeled myself
from the floorboards, why he did that.
"To make them feel good."
It was w/ this logic that Ray convinced me
to get a lap dance w/ Cocoa.
This was 9 hrs after my encounter w/ Darlene.
"Batman would do it.
George Jones would do it."
"Alright."
Cocoa's near 200-lbs & hurtin'
my legs in the joint's private loft.
"Am I hurting you?" she asked.
"No ma'am."
She rubbed nipples like
library pencils across my lips.
She told me to misbehave
so I kissed her breasts.
My legs were aching, the music
was giving me a headache,
and outside were monsters.

my educational curve.

My ol man said this 'bout the Ashtabula Harbor:
"All the bars got the smell of piss in 'em
from the sewers backing up.
That's why there's always a lot of
problems down there.
Men become like dogs,
smellin' each other's piss, & they get mean."
Joe's Coffee Shack rested at
the top of a slight crest—
the *Mansion on the Hill*, Springsteen would
say—& it acted as a safe port for
those escaping all the piss-vapors
dizzily swirling towards the
rural counties of Heaven.

Joe's Coffee Shack's interior was stunt-doubled
into an upscale NY flophouse living room.
Just the skeletal needs.
No music. No extra chatter. No laptops.
No mochagrandeswithsoymilkfilm&ashotofvanillatogo.
Just the smells of waxen old men,
cheap coffee & donuts, & that's all.
The bare bones.
Joe's was for nearly-ghost men
that didn't want to drink booze
at the VFW mid-morning to
mid-afternoon.
These guys—mostly vets or the estranged—
drank black coffee, smoked Winstons, occasionally
grated silver flakes off instant lottos,
& played cribbage.
They had tournaments there.
It was a family business—
Hard-o-hearin' ol man, tender mom,
a Bruiser Brody-ish son, a couple
squeaky-clean daughters, etc.

Ryan & I, during our half-hearted attempts
at searchin' for jobs, would stop by & chat
w/ one of the daughters, Chris.
Chris turned me onto Hesse & Steinbeck.
In fact, she was the 1st person
I'd met to recommend writers.
That felt good after all the teachers
I'd had that didn't give 2 shits
'bout me.
Chris supplied the joint w/ all the
1,000+pieces jigsaw puzzles.
A testimony to her patience.
The family superglued 'em &
tacked 'em all up like trophies
or portraits.
She had a degree in Anthropology,
& had worked at the History museum
'til the bumper-car commute drove
her nuts.
So now she just helped out her folks
& played Frisbee-golf on the weekends
w/ her beau.

Ryan & I played cribbage
during our several recesses.

Once, Ryan got a game goin' w/
the cribbage champ's son, Rocky Jr.—
the crowd around the table was thick w/ Old Spice
& Buckeye discounts & hidden war horrors—
& Ryan nearly beat the kid 'til the ol man
(that sneaky sparrow, that NASCAR-mustached soothsayer)
cupped his hand & whispered,
in a presidential advisory way,
for the boy to change his final pegs.

girls & their dads.
for my Father-in-Law.

It was a late school night &
me & Randy were hidden behind
an oak (or an elm or some big tree)
when all of a sudden I saw this
large white blur of a man—
picture George "The Animal" Steele
in solitary confinement, suddenly let go—
come chargin' at me.

This was Tonya's ol man.
Her brother-in-law saw us hidden
outside, in the shadows, when he
drove by. So he told Daddy.
After ½ a mile of runnin', Pops
grabbed me as I tried
to get into my car.
He pulled me out & gave me
a couple kicks to the ribs
as a 10% tip.

He tossed Randy, who'd finally caught
up w/ us, into the open car door.

Seems like this happened a lot,
back then.

I remember walking off of
Geneva-on-the-Lake's strip—
the strip all hussied-up w/ its
big carnival lights, cheap slushies,
mad bikers & constant swarm of
tourists & locals enjoyin' the brief spotlight—
& findin' Adrianne's dad poundin' beats
on my ol Buick w/ a chunk of branch
he had busted off a nearby pine.

I told him to stop it & he
just kept going.
So I approached him &
promised him campaign-pledges
of trouble if he didn't cut it out.

His friend held him back—
like a rabid poodle w/ a
bad perm job.

My pals backed away.

The full moon reflected on a
still Lake Erie.
Its lights shone on us like
a new form of radiation:

blue, quiet, & very nuts.

the lost years.

Ray usually had some cash.
His ol man had died
in a factory accident or was
beheaded in a car crash.
Whatever happened, Ray & his mom
got a semi-cozy pension or
a payoff.
Plus, Ray had epilepsy, & he
got disability checks for that.
So he had money
compared to the rest of
us burn-outs, us greasers.
Ray paid for the weed then
Kevin, Pete, & gang
would go fetch it.
The general alibi when they
came back w/ a mini-stash
was they got ripped off.
That's why there's only an ⅛
when there should've been
a ¼.
Really, they were pinching.

I didn't tell Ray.
I didn't like Ray much.
He was a hanger-on.
He was a burr on the side
of our group.
But all the dope was free
for me, since I provided
the place to smoke it—
my mother's place.
She had her own worries &
really didn't care much.

That's how it went.

Everyone had some role
in the main event of
gettin' stoned.

They were, however, a
nefarious group.
A gaggle of pirates.
In addition to tablespoonin'
Ray's weed, they'd demand that
he smoke a few bowls
w/ 'em.
Severance pay, if ya want,
for gettin' the dope.
The gang had all the
loyalty of drinkin' birds—
always teeter-tottering,
always laughin' behind
someone's back.

Things went on like this
for a couple years,
the lost years.
The defroster didn't
work in those years.
Those years were warmed
in a marijuana-incubator.
It was a comfortable blurriness
that grew roots.

2 things got me outta it, though.
The first was my lungs began
to shit-out on me.

You see, I have asthma & hadn't
been takin' care of 'em.
Also, I accidentially inhaled
some silicone mist at the
injection-press factory
where I worked 3rd shift.
I felt my lungs being coated
in that chemical-fog crap.
Like breadin' a chicken breast.
Or paintin' fingernails.

The second thing was the time
we were gettin' high at my place:
there were 6 of us squished
into my lil room with the door
& windows closed to keep
the smoke in: a dope sauna.

We were in there just
talkin' & listenin' to music—inside
the Wicked Witch's filthy crystal ball
all covered w/ flyin' monkey shit—
when Ray
suddenly
flopped over
& off the chair.
Like he'd died.

Then he started shakin' all
over the place—
a runaway bumper car,
a fish outta water,
an electrocution,
crashin' into everything
around 'im.

I didn't know what to do,
I'd never seen this happen
to anyone before—so I held
his head & tried to calm
his body.
I asked the other guys to
lend me a hand & they all
took off as if he were a leper
w/ leakin' abrasions.

So I told 'em to fuck 'emselves &
continued to cradle Ray's head
as if it were an egg inches away
from the skillet. Eventually,
he relaxed & seemed
to be alright.

But I was stoned & nervous & didn't
want an epileptic kid havin' another
seizure, or worse, dyin' from
somethin' unknown, so I
called an ambulance.

As the ambulance traveled 30 minutes
through the dark & desolate back roads,
its red & white lights briefly grazin' the
Hitchcock-ish woods, Ray kept
talkin' bout his hat—
where was his hat?
A broken record.

He continued this crap even when
the EMTs had arrived & kept tryin'
to go back to my room & I kept
blockin' 'im 'cause that's where

the smoke was & that's
where my plants were—
2 dozen lil plants—all growin'
for me, all achin' for the artificial sun
in my closet.
So I managed to keep Ray outta my room
& convinced 'im to go w/ the EMTs.
He did, but he was bitchin' & moanin'
the whole time.

10 minutes later,
the crew came back.
They want to know what happened.
They saw the ambulance, man.

Well, fuck 'em—thanks
for stayin'.

My one regret later on 'bout
this was that I didn't
bust their teeth in.
Some friends.

Well, the Dust Bowl
marijuana depression
began to clear
& I started to
cleave myself outta
that mess.

I began to dig into literature
like an Archaeologist w/
poison ivy.
And I began to substitute booze
for dope.

It was 'bout 5 years after those
thugs left me alone with shaky Ray
that I saw 'em at a bar near
downtown Cleveland.
It was around 1pm & I was drinkin'
between classes & in walks
the ol mob—

their arms were littered w/
Nazi tattoos & they had
all the Barbie accessories to
match: bald heads, suspenders, boots,
13-month-pregnancy beer guts.
Even the kid brothers I remembered
orbitin' around us back then had
swastikas, like rashes, on their necks
& arms.

I talked w/ 'em briefly &
that was too much.

They're bruisers & bums &
I don't want what they're sellin'.

the currents of love.

Our love story didn't begin
w/ your foreign exchange
student transfer from
France to here—
w/ me pumpin' your gas
in between thunkin' dents
outta bumpers & studyin'
engineering on the sly,
whisperin' sweet Yankee nothins
into your un-cauliflowered ears.

There wasn't a mutated
Giant Gila Monster coaxin'
broken transit, lickin' the air
for human entrees, while
jaywalkin' the Soapbox
Derby Dragsters into the bushes
w/ ragged Beach Boy surf pop
shadowin' us innocent hoods—
cherry soda hoods, greasers
that graduate, get married,
& are yo-yo-ed
back & forth by a bloated
Stalin-ish sheriff that keeps
buzzin' the red phone 'bout
assorted emergencies.

We weren't wallpapered
sock-hoppers blitzin'
the barn floors to
Jonestown ballads—
And the Lord said, Laugh children
laugh...
There was a mushroom,
a sad lil mushroom.
A meadow ready to cry...

Nah, our story begins w/ me
chokin' on a Sugar Daddy
outside a display window
stuffed w/ cartoon inflatables
slowly losin' their air.
Scenes jump-rope:
a zombie flick, a small hill w/ tons
of kids tossin' rocks,
pillagin' trash sites.

Then the moment—
the audience will realize it,
Louis & Ella croonin' hypnotics
in the background:
Love.
Your legs cricket-rubbin', violin-solo
on mine. We're both half-naked—
bed sheets consumin' our bottom
halves: Sears models, the merman
& mermaid. And you tell
me about the 3 months you spent
visitin', every day, even on Sundays,
this schizophrenic who fire-bugged
himself (doin' the protestin'
Buddhist monk thing) into
a human scab.
You stayed by this gauzed mummy's
bedside: a man you barely knew,
yet had arranged an Alcatraz escape
from his Mesopotamian asylum &
planned to do the Thoreau bit:
a trailer, some woods, a pond—
& then he fell, in a very
anti-Disney ending, for
a stripper after his
recovery.

At that time, I was
Ray-Charles-twitchin',
Emperor-Hirohito-horse-racin'
towards vague comfort
in Mormon Heaven, level #1:
where the beer is cheap,
the bartender is slow, &
the food is always overcooked.

That was my goal—
the least amount of effort;
a mealworm slow dance
w/ life—
and why not?

No one returned my kindness.
No gal, that is, until you.

patience.

It was as if the train engineer—
like the school bus driver,
so many years back, who'd threaten
to wait "No Matter
How Long It Takes"
for us to shut up—
had nothing to look forward to
beyond a TV dinner of
stale mashed potatoes,
thin Salisbury steak,
mangled cherries, & possibly
Hogan's Heroes if there
wasn't a game on.
Or maybe he simply decided
to nearly stop the
train convoy
because some hobblin' drunkard
in the last town stood by the tracks—
like a forgotten civic relic of misguided
defiance—w/ both
middle fingers flung high.

I waited 2 or so minutes, enough
time for a song 'bout
loneliness & love
to piss me off, then I pulled
down the gravel non-road
next to the tracks.
To save face, mainly.
To let those behind me believe
I know the Panama Canal away from
any captive circumstance.

The trees began to contort
into failed ballerinas &
inhibit light from reaching

the daffodils & weeds that
were blitzing the gravel briquettes.

I continued until the trail became impassable.
My truck got wedged
between 2 thick roots, &
lacking an axe or proper teeth
to hack/chew thru 'em,
I made my way by foot.
The forest floor was heavy
w/ insects—an entomologist eager
to show friends his collection,
arms pregnant w/ several trays,
trips over a sleeping beagle &
spills the bugs all over the carpet—
but I kept going.
What had started as a small trickle
of liquid, a neighbor washing his car
in the driveway, was soon all around me.
It was a wide, light green creek
w/ specks of purple & maroon
drifting along like
clotted boaters on a popular lake.
I waded forward.
I almost reached the end.
The creek was the warm bed
on a December morn w/ a slight
breeze burrowing thru a crack
in the window; the sun cutting past
curtains to cook an exposed leg.
Then I heard a voice,
a talk radio, high on morphine,
Burroughs in a Lazy Boy voice
say:

"It's just juice, doll. Some grapefruit,
kiwi, oranges, celery, strawberries,

& some prunes. You'll never
get cancer here.
It's a constant 72 degrees here."

The woman was the stuff of
Greek myth—gorgeous & packed
w/ mystery.

I should have asked questions
like: "What are you?" or
"How did you get here?"
But as she swam near & began
to examine me w/ her
juice fingers, & a couple of
her friends appeared to offer backup,
I figured the other motorists
were probably wearin' thin whatever
topics, glares, cigarettes, they had
while waitin' for the train.

Me? I don't want cancer.

born again, and again.

Sometimes it might take
several falls from grace for
a man to get up
& learn.

Take for instance my 2nd cousin,
Lloyd. I believe his heavy drinking
began while he & my grandfather were
birthing a new roofing company down
in Tennessee.
Lloyd & my granddad would soak up
their share of booze
& become familiar w/ the
indigenous locals.
The stories—of Lloyd's dose
of the crabs, Wilma's
aquarium-moss green teeth,
& my grandfather nearly being molested
by a truck of a woman running a
Pon Farr Fever—have matured
into family mythology &
still reach me as an adult.

So, Lloyd began to drink
earlier & earlier until he didn't
need an alarm clock to
buzz his brain into consciousness,
the impulse for beer beat
the clock to it.

This is how I remember him as a kid:
a kinda bloated, reddy, Hacksaw Jim Duggan
w/ blue foam bra around a Milwaukee's Best.

This is how he almost died.

His liver punched out
to cirrhosis & he was put
on dialysis.

I was betting he'd die.
We all were.

But he managed to quit boozin',
started to attend A.A. meetings,
& his liver—bless its meaty lil
regenerative skills—began to heal.

If only it ended here:
the CBS Thanksgiving special where
Dolly Parton goes home w/ Kenny Rogers
& they produce a legion of
new country singin' babies...

Instead, they'll both start acting careers & get distracted
until Lloyd finds his wife at home, already half-stewed,
w/ a fifth of whiskey in front of her.

And an empty seat next to her.

incomplete metamorphosis.

His daily medication count
was 37 pills.
That was 37 different pills
to deal w/ diabetes, high blood pressure,
bad liver, depression, etc.
Some pills were just on
the list to balance the
after effects—the body's seismic
utterances to pioneering tablets.

So his golden days became one long
run on sentence, a traffic blur,
a winter storm.

The new holidays that broke
the monotonous stream were
doctors' visits & the prompt
assignment of
better pills.

The meds made him a jerk,
altering his behaviors, manufacturing
a *Lifetime* mini-series based on
Jekyll & Hyde.

But he'd always been an ass.
At the brown-banana age of 77,
he'd managed to alienate all
of his friends & nearly all of
his family.

Almost everyone but his wife.

It didn't suprise me when
she called & told me he
had turned into a

large multi-vitamin.

He was just a 230-lb pill
laying next to the couch.

I was the one that
suggested we move him onto
the front lawn &
put up the 25¢
vitamin drink sign.

You just have to bring
your own glass.

a little past midnight.

"The earth died screaming,
while I lay dreaming of you." Tom Waits

The moon reflected a bright blue light
onto the water, onto the beach &
onto all the people there.

I was there, too. It must've
been a party.

Suddenly, w/out warning or threats,
the moon just dropped from
the sky—like a coin
into a slot machine.

We all waited for some
explanation, for some
instructions.

Nothing happened for
several minutes, then
the waves grew angry &
choppy & atop the waves
were strange creatures:
they had the stern, stereotyped faces
of worn-out librarians
sorting late books.

Their bodies resembled sea lions
w/ thick, large scales
all over their backs
& limbs.

The sky was already dark &
the only light came from
these monsters—these

bookwormish harpies—
like mad, fluorescent light bulbs.

They began to devour
those of us on the shore.
Many just stood in shock &
waited to be appetizers.

I ran to a phone booth
on the beach, closed
the glass door &
tried calling you.

I was going to warn you,
but you never answered.

welcome aboard!

Bar counter strangers sit like tombstones
& might gasp jokes
about the 5th floor between
cigarette smoke. They hide
their mental struggles & pretend
this is prenatal care
for a new friendship.

The 5th floor psych ward
rests atop Ashtabula hospital
like a small derby hat on
a mutant-sized head—
uncomfortable & awkward.

This is where everyone
in the area comes during
their psychological transitions.

This is where I came
after a walk in the woods
with a long rope looking
for the shortest branch.

Give 'em your belts
& shoelaces—there's
no successful suicides
here.

This was my intro.
I was given the realtor tour
around then settled
into a routine as fluid as a
divorced woman w/ 4 frozen
vertebrates & 36 rat terriers
sharing her kitchen.

I first met 3 therapists, like Cerberus

guarding the door
to psychological wellness.
They weren't fightin' over
a Spartan's leg bone, they were
competing to analyze us.

They all had peer-reviewed
papers to write.

Their boss, the resident shrink, was
Dr. Kim—a man w/ all the bedside
empathy of Dracula at a blood bank;
a business man / bounty hunter after
Caine in *Kung-Fu*;
a cold, stoic robot willing
to soak our health insurance to
its last percolated drop.

But there was a nite-lite of
mental well being that resided
in the neighborhood art therapist.
She gave me unlimited access
to her supplies.

I painted a dozen pictures
of Jackie O.

The other residents were a
sad group—like Boxcar Willie
driven mad by trains.

There was a motorcycle accident
Evel-Knievel-failure head injury case—
a semi-beefy hoss of a man
that was meteorologist kind

& bugged—almost horse-flied—
by his short term memory collapses.

But he was a decent
ping pong player.

There was a former
creative spirit—
an early 40s wrinkled-blouse-
waiting-years-for-the-dryer-with-
yellowed-gray-hair-from-all-
the-cigarette-smoke-in-all-the-bars-
remnants-of-beauty-worn-like-erosion-
from-all-the-abusive-men-drugs-and-
probably-childhood-molestation-
tired woman.

I thought about hookin'
her up w/ my dad.

There was a post-or mid-menopause
frizzed blond woman w/ severe depression—
w/ heartache from a recent divorce or death
& a great disconnect from her kids, even
though they would give her souvenir t-shirts,
w/ German shepherds or collies on 'em,
from all the places they'd
traveled to.

She hated animals.

I seem to remember some
bearded, catatonic men—
like children of Bigfoot caught
in that strange limbo between
thought & speak.

They were heavily shackled
to medication &
rarely seen—
those poor, waddling specters.

After 9 days, I felt no big difference.
I refused drugs & was advised
to see a therapist
once a week.

Maybe I just needed
a break.
Maybe we all need
breaks.

I do miss my temp foster family.
I hope they're doing better.

I see them in a lot of faces.

We meet one another at
strange curves in the road,
or at various stops.

I try to value
all the visits.

saturday afternoon.
for Bates

In the 34th hour of
my 40-hr community service stretch,
the Reverend makes me
wash his new Ford
while he sits on a lawn chair
& watches.
He's soon joined by Martin—
I'll learn his name in
my 36th hour while
unloading desks w/ 'im.
He's not a criminal—
maybe a union employee
to the Lord; I'm a scab.
Martin's younger than me:
fatter, nerdish, clean shaven.
I've got an 11-day beard, and
am wearin' a U.S.S. Cod shirt—
the same one I was arrested in.
I envision takin' him out
afterwards, gettin' him drunk
& encouragin' him to steal
a flower pot, an American flag
& a sign that says
Welcome to Unionville.

They just stare at me when
their conversations nosedive.
The Reverend yells at me
for putting towels near a water puddle.
They may have a
clearer phone line to Christ
than me, but I know what
makes another human being uncomfortable.

I haven't wanted to slug
someone so much for 2 days.

the mud puddle.

The first thing you see
when you walk into
The Red Light Tavern is
a map of the U.S.—so
sun bleached & brittle
that the names
of the states,
of the cities, have
all disappeared.

The second thing you see
is the barstools, like board
game pegs forming a burnt-out
Lite Brite square;
molding together a
small, incestuous community.

It wasn't fate, really, that
caused Charlie & Mona
to meet.
It was just random
placement, like
refrigerator magnets.

They both drank Bud Lite
& they both nodded,
arhythmically, to
The Oak Ridge Boys
on the jukebox.

And they both listened
to the same nightly stories—
wobbly fireside chats told
to them & the other
bar regulars by
various insane townsfolk.

Stories like wet concrete that
eventually harden into
memory.

Those that remain in this
small town, in this small bar,
have multiple problems & hang-ups
that climb like poison ivy
onto a flophouse.

The few women no longer resemble
barflies, but rather a new
variation, a new species:
mud puppies—
those nearly extinct salamanders—
w/ their thin skin showing
passersby all the baggage,
the luggage, the carry-ons
& the accessories
that come w/ 'em.

The men just stare desperately
like anonymous insects in
a Venus Flytrap.

That's how Charlie & Mona met.
No Hollywood courtship,
no higher expectations, just
reduced choices &
neighboring bar stools.

So they got married.

They went through three houses
like Mr. Monopoly w/ dementia
& went bankrupt.

Charlie's ol man
bailed 'em out of
financial woe.

The kicker was Mona
had someone else's
baby—a square-headed baby
that curiously resembled
Boris Karloff:
always just
staring at you—

distant & desperate.

contributions.

Certain things you can
predict with ease:

we'll destroy ourselves w/
chemicals & war, then
become slaves to evolved ants;
it'll rain somewhere
on the planet in
April;
and that elephant
at the Medieval Faire
will flip out—
stampeding thru humans
like King Kong putting out
cigarettes.

I'm guessing 2 years.

Any intelligent animal would.
Rototilling thier own footprints
over & over
in the same small circle.

I'm just glad I got to ride it
before that happens.

foreign policy is the name of the show.

The Disaster Family—a current
amalgamation of the Kennedys courting
the *Lost in Space* clan—experiences
a slew of natural/social catastrophes
(avalanche, earthquake, volcano,
civil war, uprisings, etc.) in each adventure.
And they have the myopic juggler's
tendency to lose a family member
in each episode.
Say, grandmother burns her legs
to candle stubs in molten lava;
the second cousin is beheaded
in a whittling mistake; the dog is
used as accidental bait to catch
a 100-ft giant squid.

These reverse, bad luck Noahs.
These poor Burgess Merediths
in *The Twilight Zone*.

That's how the series goes.
Until they're all that's left.

like father, like son.
(The relatability of stories.)

I was telling my dad that
one of my best decisions,
next to getting married, was
not hitting that reverend when
he over stepped the
community service boundaries
& wanted me to fold his
skivvies in his bedroom.
I didn't punch him, I just left.
I did, later on, drink 10 beers
& shovel 2 tons of gravel
to get the mad out.

My ol man told me you can
always walk away.
Sometimes that's the best thing:
"Like the time I was sittin'
at this junior-mafia roundtable,
with these guys quizzin' me
about where I buy my drugs.
I was stoned at the time,
which helped, but there was this
gorilla poundin' his fist into
his hand like he was
tenderizin' steaks.
Then this stripper I knew came
over to me and whispered:
'Bob, these guys probably won't hurt
you, but they did cause a man
to go crazy last week.'
So I just stood up & walked out.
Tho' I did duck behind all the trees
for the next mile
until I reached my car."

ants & generals.

Part 1.
First they sent in
the scouts.
And when they found
the half-open package
of Certs on the window sill,
they brought in
the rest.
Like a pioneer caravan
headin' towards a young California,
the ants came in waves.
We squished the ones that
bypassed the chemical, roadside
Bates motels w/ green plastic
Army generals.
Patton ended up gettin' a couple,
though Clay was the new
insect-equivalent Buffalo Bill.

Two days after all the
flattened dead ants were slung
over their living comrades' shoulders,
the queen ant came
to visit me.

Maybe she was going to
call a cease-fire or
offer to pay the water bill
if we let them alone.

I stepped on her twice
& tossed the body
in the trash w/ coffee grinds
& eggshells before she could
say her position.
No U.N. debate club here.

Part 2.
Lust is a lot like that.
Ant infestation, I mean.
A few stray thoughts can carpool
to much larger ideas &
schemes.
And your heart becomes
a hive to hidden agendas,
plans, & desires.
And it's only when your girl finds
the *Erotic Survivor* video & you feel
like a 14-yr-old boy who just stole a picture
of his aunt topless, that you realize
the impact.
Say, you haven't rented a porn in 500+ days
& you only watched
10 minutes of this one
& if it was yours
you'd bury it in the backyard w/ the rest.
But it isn't yours.
You've given up strip clubs, dancers,
Penthouse mags, dubious massage parlors,
& now you give this up, too.
Doin' it in 2-yr installments.
Cuz forever is easier
reached in pieces. And love
is more valuable than some
big-titted Indian broads clammin'
it up w/ grungy punk gals.

dog walking.

My wife recently started walking dogs.
Yesterday, this one dog, Jenny, had
cornered Trin in its house—
in front of the door, snarling,
growling & shaking.
Trin called her boss & waited
to be rescued, the whole time
holding Jenny back w/ a stool.
A practice test towards
her lion taming degree.

She was nervous afterwards, naturally,
so I walked w/ her & the next dog—
a fat orange clump of flesh
named Grace.
Grace was a mastiff that
looked like a Jim Henson
design flaw.
But she was a cool dog,
so this gave me a chance to
tell Trin about a dog that
chased me once:
"Me & my friend Kenny were riding
our bikes on Rt. 84, when outta the
blue, this huge black lab started barking
like mad & zeroed in on us.
When it ran across the road
(cats'll look both ways, but dogs rarely do)
it got hit hard by a Chevy truck & its
back legs were waffled
to the pavement.
Its yelps were horrible.
Hell's soundtrack.
So the poor thing tried crawlin'
back home, draggin' chunks of flesh
that used to be its legs.

Me & Kenny stopped our bikes
& watched.

You remember that house—
where Mark H. died.
He had cancer all over his body.
He was sliced in the back by a
Vietcong soldier & I remember asking him
to see the scar when I was
a kid.
Well, I thought I saw his son, Jeremy,
behind the house the other day
when we passed by.

I wanted to stop & say I was sorry
'bout his ol man, but I don't
think it would've mattered."

relations.

Thanksgivin' morn,
traveling down a clear highway:
no music, few clouds—
all the moods of the neighboring
motorists are revealed by their speeds—
when I hear,
like a novice druid practicing
his one line over&over&over
for the big chant
tomorrow evening:
"Your engine coolant level is low,
immediate maintenance is required."
I threaten my car
(I call it KITT when it misbehaves)
"Just one more time,
one more warning."

After 37 minutes of its self-diagnosis—
a mechanical wolf cry for help—
I crack the speedometer plastic
& stab all the numbers,
all the gauges, w/ a screwdriver.

A few days ago, sitting—arms
pressed inward like the girl in
Munch's *Puberty* painting—on
the edge of my bed:
it's 1am & I'm watching a
matriarch hyena cub devour her siblings.
Then, next, a mother lion's
mouth foaming, legs drunk—all because of
an unruly cobra living next door.
She eventually manages a half-circle
(how long it takes, the viewer doesn't
know) & she smells her cubs, dead.
She lies down beside them, blind.

My dreams that mornin'
weren't furnished w/ campaigns
of reform towards cobras &
hyena children—it's their nature.
Just as all kids need the chance
to die. That's what Mike told me
when we eyed a swarm of
young adventurers trotting to
the Grand River.
No, my dreams were of the old.

Submerged times when my grandfather
would take me, 10-12 yrs old, to the
clubs w/ him.
All those men—vets from a couple
different wars—gabbin' about
daily events, relations; their asses formin'
into the small, round shape of the barstools.
They're all dead by now, or very close.
Even Rudy.
Rudy was the kind goblin child
of post-60s loneliness w/ an insatiable
urge for Kessler's—*The Urge:*
that eager student always
raisin' its hand in any A.A. lead;
that exit ramp towards wrappin'
a car 'round a tree or wipin' out a family.
Rudy postponed this inevitability, as
most of the men did, w/ early drinking.
The bars were usually full before 11am.
Rudy would give me his spare change—
change left over from a beer & shot—
if I could name X-amount of correct state capitals.
I got a couple bucks a week outta him.
But it's been so many years since
Rudy tossed me dimes & quarters

for a shred of education.
This was before I had gotten into the habit
of arguing politics & religion w/ a
mashed-potatoes-not-entirely-ready
shape of an old man.
An ex-History prof, I think.
A guy who had a museum honoring fellas
under The Articles of Confederation & a bar
boastin' the largest selection of booze
in the world. I told 'im, after
he said my sister's disability was
caused by the devil: "I'll give ya
that 5th heart attack!"
My grandfather walked in then—
Praise God!—& escorted me
to another bar.

I was doing side jobs, roofing w/ my grandfather.
We stopped at The Eagles for a couple drafts.
There was Rudy.
More withered; a frozen fugitive Viking
found in the Himalayas, now sippin' Blatz
in an Ohio pub.
I said hello & he started into me—
noticin' the tar smears & fiberglass
kernels movin' in w/ arm hair—
about my failure to do anything
w/ my life.

"I will. I will. I'm just helpin' my grandpa now."
"Bullsheet. Yer wastin' yer life."
My grandfather, not an empath, but
able to hear my responses increase
in straining tolerance, pulled me
to yet another bar—just as he will
in another year.

my mother's end of it.

Part 1.
Life wasn't a political campaign trip
w/ Mayor McCheese after the
divorce: all Happy Meals & good times.

My ol man moved into a
mildewed caboose
shoved like a peg from a
giant's coordination test
into the gravelly side of a hill.
He took baths in a pond
w/ the bass & bluegills nibbling
his toes & fingers.

Back home,
our dogs de-domesticated,
ate the cat & began to shit
piles on the floor.

The fleas saw the neon vacancy sign
& brought all their relatives—
they were all over us like a
dot-to-dot drawing; like
cartoon measles.

We were the growth in
the gutter: muddy & string-beany
& tired from the weight of
the water.

Lindsay, at this time,
was a child
of The Hulk.
Her disorder, under stress, allowed
her tantrums to explode like
a dozen feet-stomping children

on plate glass during
square dancing finals.
Small animal torture.
Thrown furniture.

My mother had it the toughest, though.

One night, a few nights after the divorce,
her non-stop, broken record, broadcast system
warning, sad siren sobs, waterfall crying, reached
my bedroom—

She had eaten half a bottle
of aspirin & all I could do
was tell her to shut up.

Some kid.

Part 2.
She took a job bartending at
Jefferson County's main biker-trash bar,
The Wooden Nickel.
It was a mealworm's paradise.
Coffee cans instead of urinals.
3,000-yr-old sawdust on
the floor, a mummy's spilled
intestines.
It wasn't a Hollywood case study
for biker movies.
I remember a wet darkness
to the place
like an armed robbery
gone bad.

Eventually,
Mom got outta that dive &

relocated to a slightly worse
hole-in-the-wall bar, The Grand Manor.

More drugs, more bikers, more trouble.

Most of the weed I inhaled, outside
of the uterus, was in my ol man's garden
& in The Manor—
a tough joint where dying brillo-pad men
picked on 8th grade boys.
A grimy place where every 5th customer
was an undercover cop.
A tourist hotspot where barflies
pulled change outta the toilets.

It was here that some crum—
an anyman, his face made for the
FBI's top 10—pulled a bow & arrow
on my mom because she'd called
the Sheriff on his disruptive ass
a few nights earlier.
So she called the cops on Robin Hood's
drunken cousin again.

He wouldn't let it slide—weeks later, he
rammed my mother's car in the bar parking lot.
Repeatedly. Like a stutterer w/ a hard sentence.

When she got off of work
around 3am, she found his
license plate stuck in her
smashed bumper
like a lonesome
valentine letter.

He got upset when the police
knocked on his door at 4am.

locals.

Part 1.
It begins like this:
a love seat collage of
prescription drug bottles—
Burroughs' stash after
Drugstore Cowboy—and a
still life painting of a
community of marijuana roaches
(a dime bag, a small clip, and an
empty bottle of Mad Dog
on the coffee table.)
It continues like this:
a couple roustabout comments
hotwired around normal ones—
thoughts orphaned outside the
cerebral cortex, blanketed in
sections of Police *Do Not Cross* tape
& dead relatives communicating via
private Ham Radio frequency:
We know who's next this year.
Who's going to die.
Ready? Write this down.
Later on, the same program
features all of her sexual adventures
on the air.

The result is this:
midnight wanderings into a
nearby graveyard, hair frizzed
like Einstein's sister w/ wet finger
stuck in the electrical socket,
asking strangers,
Do I know you?;
alienating her husband;
calling various relations,
before the phone is tapped,

& announcing, *I'll be dead in
two hours. Fuck off!*
This gets her a night,
all expenses paid, in the
county jail.

Part 2.
Nearly every city, every business
district, has them—
the local nut-jobs. The whackos.
The mad. The mythological Pans
with itchy balls, swelled crotches,
and many formulas on life.

It's a different viewpoint
now knowing one's origin.

On my work-street, there's—

The Oracle: a forty-something, bi-racial man
decked out in bright sequin dresses, sea cucumber/
jester caps, always burying clothes & food
behind iambically-abbreviated homes like
an ADHD diagnosed squirrel;
the result of a pocketful of LSD in a thunderstorm,
or from lapping a gal's neck who had used
an FDA-rejected mosquito spray.

Armadillo Woman: a very staunch Democrat
shelled in Pro-Choice/Pro-Women/Pro-Animal/
Pro-Anti-Murder buttons & pins; corsaged
by a decomposing neck brace—turned brown
like the forgotten head of lettuce in
the crisper drawer—which
has become a thick scarf
shingling (like a hooded clitoris)

her large breasts where she
banks her wet cash.

Hot Dog Lady: an ex-hot dog vendor
who still hasn't lost the quick-skips—
over stadium steps, over concrete slabs
to deliver those meats—to run errands;
she is the hurrying Hermes
of Cleveland Heights.

My aunt is training to be
one of these noticeable apparitions.

She could've lived in
Larry's (my girl's brother)
apartment building—
a low-rent, Lego-bricked box
stashed w/ tenants
Siamese-twinned to disabilities,
dope problems, mental defects, etc.

The woman above would
Bride of Frankenstein goosestep
from kitchen to toilet
as frequently as
cell division.

Other peripheral neighbors would
develop trade school skills
in meth labs and walking stick
limps & aches.

The neighbor below Larry
had sensitive ear infections of
The Six Million Dollar Man
& would complain about
the box fan humming, the

microwave buzzing,
flies fucking—

I imagine my aunt behind
this man when he pokes his head out of a
fourth floor window and yells—one of
the old men in the balcony from *The Muppets Show*—
to Larry, 3pm, just getting
out of his car in the
parking lot,
"Go to bed!"

"king ghidorah on my clitora!

For women who want that
King Ghidorah feeling but
don't want to date
the King."

That's what the box said.
Beneath this late-night-aimed slogan
was a picture of the three-headed
dragon that used to bump
heads w/ Godzilla & Mothra
in Tokyo.

Barb found the box next
to a dumpster at
her job.

It was a prototype shown
—and rejected—at the
Pittsburgh New Sexual & Kitchen-Usable
Appliances Convention.

The device, she discovered,
left its users partially invalid
for several hours—
the mistaken short-sightedness of marrying a
metallic schlong & a garbage disposal.
Barb lay stunned on her
bedroom floor, like a tropical fish
dynamited out of a coral reef,
reading the various attachments
listed on the box
as a means of pawning clarity.
"Tongue types included:
Special Candy-Button Romance.
Cat's Tongue Denial.
Lazy Butter Knife.

And introducing
the long awaited
Hydra attachment."

A Lionel Train blipped within
the corridors of her brain
& the stops it made were
reminders to lock the bedroom door
when her parents were home.

resurrection.

They heard the story of Lazarus
while in the womb, so
when their dog—the one
their father had shot to teach
them a lesson in
ownership & responsibility—
had de-thawed from its
winter death & arose
to greet them & Spring
w/ half its skull exposed,
brain smiling w/ new activity:
they cheered for Jesus!

The father led the dog
away from the children &
gave it another bullet
and a deeper grave.

her name was lust.

Part 1.
My tree, my home, was
next to a large reddish/brown
miles-high mansion.

There weren't many leaves
on my tree, less than a
hundred, but they were
all clumped together like
a puffy flat top haircut.

It was raining hard &
the leaves provided me
w/ enough protection.
The fat rain dropped heavily
onto the concrete ground—
near me, but not on me.

Still, I wanted more cover
& I remembered a woman
down the road that had
a big, blue tarp.

So I left my tree, stepped
into the flood of rain &
traveled a hundred yards
or so—then came back
for my socks.

While I was putting on my socks,
I noticed a figure sitting
on a wooden chair inside
the mansion's patio.

He was dressed in a thick red robe
& had the hood pulled over
his face.

When the figure noticed me,
he leapt through the glass doors—
without breaking them—&
came upon me.

I've seen enough episodes of
Kung Fu to know how to twist &
use an attacker's momentum
against him.

I did this & it worked.
I had the assailant on
the ground.
He shook his right hand quickly,
punched it into my body &
took out my left lung.
It was full of cancer.

Part 2.
I found myself in an auditorium—
or at least half of an auditorium—
its walls curving toward a figure
seated on a throne.

I couldn't make him out clearly,
but on each side, along the walls,
stood several individuals
watching me.

I walked confidently to the
seated figure, passing
the sideline of people
w/out a second glance.

As I neared the figure—whom
I still could not see—a red headed
woman stepped into my path
from a hidden closet.

The figure spoke in an even & booming
voice: "You can tempt him, after
I tempt him."

She didn't listen & grabbed my
hand & led me into the closet.
She was naked now &
I could not resist.

As I began to climax, I saw
two individuals in the middle of
the room—a man like a distorted vampire
w/ slick black hair kissing a rather
ordinary woman.

As he pulled away from the kiss,
revealing his sharp jagged teeth,
I saw him sucking a
thick white cloud
out of her.

cut down the trees & name roads after them.

The drive out there was a
constant blur of trees—
the sun peeking through
in slices, like a 8mm film projector
being juggled & always catching bits
of the audience's heads.

The Oldsmobile—2 yrs before
its sad Friday night stint at
the local demolition derby—smelled
of spilled coffee, spilled beer,
spilled joints, & the car seat's
inner yellow-Zingerish upholstery cushions
would stick to your clothes
like burrs or radioactive fleas.

We were going to our
parents' friends' place.
These mad Thoreau frontiersmen & women
that didn't write nature essays, but instead,
perimetered themselves w/
marijuana plants & cages
full of bluish dogs—
like backwoods Moreau scientists
farting around w/ wolf, dingo, fox,
coyote DNA for that
just right combo-platter
of American pet.

Their kids were a beefy-broth mix
of scabs & dirt.
They were the hardy children
of Jim Bowie, of Daniel Boone,
of Abraham Lincoln—
these kids of the 1800s
wrapped in aluminum foil,

put in the fridge, forgotten about,
then de-thawed in 1983.

We would get so lost in
the woods that any sign of civilization—
a bike track, a beer bottle, a telephone line—
was a blessing.
And when we'd find a dirt road
or trail, we'd have a sense of
great relief

& gutpunch disappointment.

another beer garden.

My mother and I were
shooting pool, doubles, at
The Bermuda Triangle, against
a typical hick (an alcoholic prop
unevenly abbreviated by failed
working stiffs, their trucks outside
swollen with equipment that hasn't
moved for 7 yrs) and his
friend or son, who became
a passive delegate when his
partner said, after my mother
played some Johnny Lee Hooker
tunes on the jukebox (*Crawlin' King
Snake,* baby): "Who played that
devil shit!?" The bartender,
with a plate tectonic revolution of
fat cells leaking over her leaf-green shorts,
two sizes too small—though she's
attractive in the face—turned
the jukebox volume up, causing large
women to pinch spacial g-spots
with their bodies, like a pagan
sock hop.

Euthanized bikers are resurrected
yawning slogans of indecision.
And the man—the standard slug
w/ an oiled Exxon hat, sleeveless
gray shirt, & tattoos drawn in
amateur-cubist style revealing unnatural
backwoods compromises—says, while
my mother
takes aim
at the eight:
"Ah, she won't make it!
Shit shot! We've won!"

I shout confidence—
he rebuts with scorn.
She sinks it and jabs
her stick into his orbit.
His gripes translate into hate.
He won't accept our victory
as the truth.
The man doubts himself—
like a human who is told by teenage aliens
that the earth is a science fair project,
and they have the schematics
and the awards to prove it.

He passes out
before I can beat the truth
into his head by combining
his right and left lobes
w/ a 19 oz. cue.

no peace in the country, either.

I could only deal w/ so many
cars lined up behind each other,
w/ so many houses & buildings stacked
right next to one another, that
I needed to see some trees
that weren't trimmed & decorated
w/ little fences or grass that
was mowed—or being mowed.

We were at my ol man's for
a birthday party & before
I went for a 3-mile trek into
some woods, he introduced me
to his biker pals.
Ron was a Sam Elliot from
Roadhouse, older biker.
He'd just had a heart attack.
And his gal, Jill, was a couple
decades younger than him.

"She seemed shy," I told my dad,
a couple weeks later when we
were catching up.

"Well, she isn't on film," he said.
Then told me how Ron & Jill
had made a sex video & given
it out to their close friends—
like a Christmas card or
something.

"The camera angles need some work.
It was a bit static," he said.
"All they had was a tri-pod.
They asked me if I'd be
the camera man for the next one."

"So what did you say?"

"I'd think about it."

flypaper waltz.

Part 1.
We almost didn't eat at
The Last Chance Restaurant
because of the smell:
something like a nursing home cafeteria
or Mr. Death's sous-chef.

The restaurant was a relic,
an anomaly, a rest stop reminder
of how things were 50 yrs back.
Indeed, a *Lost World*—without
the brontosaurus burgers or
pterodactyl-egg omelets—
w/ a moderate brunch
selection & a nearly UFO devotion
to lighthouses.

There was a repetitive lighthouse stamp,
or stutter, border-patrolling
the wallpaper & the customers.

Even the light switches had
a lighthouse design.

Part 2.
Our dining neighbors were old,
the lingering dead.
The kinda people who'll watch anything
on the restaurant TV
—ice skating, an execution—
rather than talk,
just talk,
to their companions.

The fruit flies, too, seemed sluggish
w/ hibernation sickness.

Their slow zigzags drifted like
a tortoise courtship into our coffee,
into our ice cream, into our talk
about past loves & no regrets.

Part 3.
I hope all my ex-flames,
& yours,
are doing fine & have
found happiness.
I want everyone to feel my
hot-tubbish contentment—

especially the waitresses & cooks here.
It seems their dreams have become
unwashed & sticky like the tiled floor
around the salad bar.

cooking class.

At the ages of
5 & 7, they were
snatching dining room chairs
from their natural habitats
& using them as
stepladders to reach
the stove.

One kid burned hamburgers
while the other harvested
flower bulbs in the backyard
for an appetizer.

Their mother was oblivious
to the lonely 2-lb box of rice
in the cupboard or
the rotting, groundmeat brain
in the fridge.

The U.S. Armed Forces Survival Manual talks
about the human spirit's need to survive:
"Our bodies are highly complex machines,
yet even when subjected to the most
harsh & degrading conditions, the will
to live can sustain the living process."

The mother did eventually
realize that she wasn't the one
ruining skillets, &
sent a co-worker from
Red Lobster to explain
to the kids the differences
between rare & done.

He used the burns on his arm
as a flow chart.

the gaps between us.

The bar's innards are sparse—
rafter beams resemble a
Brontosaurus rib cage &
its population is small &
spread out, like cheap butter
on toast, or prototype
hair plugs on Kojak.

The bands share the stage,
between set changes, w/
The Iraq Veterans Against
The War.
Leonard, Cleveland's chapter
president, is a hip, cool,
Bob Marley w/ neater dreads
that talks, abbreviatedly, about
his 20-yr stint in the Marines,
about his time in Iraq,
& about his PTSD.

He does a good job ignoring
the applause at the
wrong spots &
the hick comments
about "preaching."

After his speech, I approach
Leonard at his table,
buy him a beer,
& tell him
I appreciate what
he's doing.

Sam's band is tuning
their instruments, so I
re-join Trin & Tom.

The band does an alright job
at rousing people.

A Kris Kristofferson look-alike, playing
the role of ye ol Wolf Man—who was
here earlier, watching close-binocular,
some girls doing sexy bumper-car
grinds—nods agreeably
to the music.

But there's a moment around
this time when things start
getting weird—like a Dave Lynch
film, an ultra-sense of
awareness; it becomes a
bull fight pre-show
tornado.

The autistic guy / ADHD fellow /
recent car accident victim near
our table becomes antsy.

There really is something
wrong w/ him.

He's big too, so now I'm
getting anxious.

He's a mound of organized meat,
a 6-ft+ pile of sliced ham given
awkward animation.
He moves in a stir-crazy, remote controlled,
asylum-maze kinda way:
from the bar to the table to the door to the stage to
the staircase, then back to the bar where he
takes off his shirt & shows the bartender his tattoos.

She's a Suicide Girl dropout w/ erratic
Egyptian-meets-white-trash hieroglyphic
tattoos—like Deli Meat's: hither & thither,
to & fro—from her neck to her calves.

Suddenly,
Sam's spotted in the stage's red light
& this causes him to look less like
Jesus feeding the multitude fish & bread,
& more like Rasputin
seismographing Godzilla's return
on guitar.
He's going nuts on the strings—
the way I'd imagine the fiddle player
in *The Devil Went Down to Georgia*;
& he starts belting out mad Hendrix
Voodoo Child.

Wolf Man is nodding faster now;
Deli Meat is a blur;
Sam's face becomes distorted
in the blood ghost light;
& we notice Leonard
arguing w/ some mildewy
Mark Twain w/ wrangled
sparrow-egg white hair
slicked back like erosion
& an unkempt Fu Manchu
dripping slow inches
towards a weak chin.

He's gotta wet washcloth
tiredness to him—
I imagine him coming to this bar for years,
hoping to
score w/ each new bartender.

They get younger &
he ages like newspaper
in the sun.
The two men start verbally jousting,
territorially pissing on each other:
Leonard's served 20 yrs,
Twain's got 5 yrs in Nam.

He's seen real action, so has he, on & on.

It keeps escalating until
Leonard finally just walks
outside. Smart move, I think.
It's Mark Twain's bar & he's
buddies w/ Deli Meat & Wolf Man.
I try to buy him a beer, but
he's been cut off.
He starts rambling on about
his time served, some racist comments,
& then I leave.
Apparently, he's suffering from PTSD, too.

Outside, I say so long to Leonard,
& wish him well.

He's all fired-up, too.

I feel bad for both of them.
They've got more in
common than they
realize.

*Lord, be w/ 'em,
be w/ 'em all.*

mother's day.

It's not just raining cats & dogs
outside, they're being
vomited from the sky.

Inside, we form an
obtuse triangle w/ our
mismatched chairs—
me, my dad, & my grandma.

We're waiting around
for the call about Ethel—
my step-grandmother—
she's dying from
pancreatic cancer.

So, somehow, in this Bermuda triangle
sorta way, we end up talking about
my ol man's adolescent girlfriends:

"Do you remember Becky, mom—
the redhead?"

"Did she have gonorrhea?"

"No, that was Cindy.
Becky told me, loudly mind you,
in Angelo's Bowling Alley, that:
'You didn't get the clap from me!!'
I'm sure she didn't get any
numbers that night."

"Probably not."

"Well, anyway, when I was buying
my 4th prescription of clap ointment,
the pharmacist, Old Man Sanders, said:

'Bob, you know you have to keep increasing
the potency of ointment for each
dose of the clap you get.
Maybe it's time you settled down,
cause you've reached
the limit."

"So, you reached your expiration date
with the clap," I said.

"Yeh, soon after that,
I met your mom."

children of divorce.

Keith's parents got divorced
before mine.
He was 11 or 12 when
his ol man got custody.
A lot of the time, Keith's
paternal grandparents—
an ancient couple: think of
the grandparents from
The Grapes of Wrath aged
3 times—would drive
us around Ashtabula
in a light brown
rustbucket Buick.

Keith was mean to them,
real mean.

He was always shouting directions
& demands at them
from the fabric-torn &
partially disemboweled
back seat.

They endured his rotten behaviors
like Job in a Taliban
nursery school.

Things got bad one day when
Keith—like a pepper stuffed
w/ dynamite—exploded on
his grandma &
choked her out.

He threw her walker aside,
pushed her against the wall,
& throttled her big, soft neck.

His grandparents didn't drive
him around after that,
I didn't hang around him
once I heard about it,
& Keith's ol man was
meaner & more distant
once that happened.

Some kids are better at
dealing w/ divorce than others.

I never choked anyone—
I only wrecked every vehicle
I could get my hands on.

current political discussions.

His great aunt had asked
him to come over & cut
the fallen tree branches
that littered the backyard.

The young man went over
one morning, unannounced, to
survey the work ahead.

The great uncle, handicapped
by dementia & diabetes, saw
someone in his yard.
So he went & grabbed his shotgun,
opened the window, took
careful aim, & shot his
nephew in the back.

The local newspapers called it
a tragedy, but mentioned that
the young man should have
called first.

saved again.

Christmas night:

Paul, the responsible Litho,
shoves past the front door—
w/ us, the most passive
of police informants, squealin'
on comic books at
the kitchen table—&
invites us to his community-pad
for a late holiday dinner.

The apartment's like
the Rebellion's last headquarters
after Hoth, complete
w/ a Furby couple &
red flags chicken-poxing
a map of the States
on a yellow wall.
Much vodka, beer, raw fish
& garlic carrots.
The cook of the carrots
is a 26-yr old red head
from eastern Lithuania
working w/ a
temp visa in Chicago.

Shove 10 beers & 3 shots
of Smirnoff in me, allow me
to stare at her
for several minutes
(unnoticed)
before hearing her say,
"I don't want to go back home;
there's no work there,"
& I'm ready to
push a ring on her finger.

Back-up support, in my mind—
she's got this near dangerous
Mary Astor from *Maltese Falcon* sneer,
can at least make decent carrots,
& probably puts out.
But I get distracted...

Nary stumbles into the kitchen
w/ a butcher knife: to saw
his arm, his head.
He's already loopy from
broad-jumpin' the stairs &
smoochin' the heater w/
his teeth & nose.
Muddy—whose original name is
too tough for us average Americans
to pronounce—sits next to me,
near the coleslaw, near
his gal, both wash-cyclin'
Pat Benatar lyrics.
Mike hits the bathroom wall,
on a mad high, w/ his fist.

In fifty minutes, I'll be choked-out;
in an hour & a half, after log-walkin'
2.7 miles over snowdrifts, ice patches,
the half-salted road— to my
friend's place—I'll ruin my rear axle
by backin' over a large cement block
at the tail end of
the driveway.

Almost 3 yrs ago, I rolled
my grandmother's Honda Civic—
midday, July something, on thick gravel—
8, 9, 10? times;

a few hundred yards, anyway.
Bill & me walked away from
the car—lookin' very much
like a mistaken Rodan egg—
w/ just sore ears, the complaints
of loose 9-irons & a
couple swipes from
floatin' glass.

Throw in a couple accidents
I didn't cause & I'll think
if there are guardian Angels,
there's probably a squadron
houndin' me & they're
most likely always askin'
for re-assignment.

modern health care.

Part 1.
He's gotta couple granddaughters, teenagers
by now, that he's never seen—
yet he's willing to donate cash to
the top scholars & best athletes
among the local Boy Scout ranks.

He was doing this last week—
standing behind a podium, walking
down marble steps, handing out
personal checks, until he
slipped & egg-cracked his
skull on the stairs.

He passed out,
laying on the floor like a
fallen Santa Claus or a sucker-punched
Blake painting.

My grandmother got his
telephone call from the hospital
around 3am.

She overcame insomnia & its
awkward partnering of
sleeping pills & low-fat ice cream
to join John at the ER.

The story pebble-skips past
the drive there to the stroll
from the parking lot to
the hospital:
"I was walking behind an
elderly Jewish couple & then
we noticed a few hoodlums
near the entrance.

I was anxious & worried until
I realized we were 2 old Jews
& one insane woman versus
4 black thugs.
I think we could've taken 'em—
& if we couldn't, they probably
realized we were poor
& had old vaginas."

Part 2.
The front of the hospital
is the *Better Homes & Garden* botanical
cheerleader you'd like to fuck—
it's a perfect place, colorful, &
that's all you notice.
Everything else is a sloppy joe.
And inside the hospital
it's a mealworm;
the potato salad you've forgotten in
the fridge; a Joan Collins robot.

Part 3.
John & my grandmother
waited 4+ hours in the
hospital hallway.
His head kept leaking blood
as he curbed consciousness
like a feral dog.
Finally, he started talking
to his hallway neighbors about
the "fucking doctors" &
their priority lists.
"Well," my grandma continued:
"this tubby nurse—a guy around
400-lbs—went & told the
doctor what John said.

So the doctor stopped whatever
she was doing—massaging hearts,
or scooping brains back in—&
came out & lectured John
about his language.
It was all too ridiculous.
Once the doctor left,
John called the blabby nurse
a wimp & a tattletale.
Then another nurse went
& told the same doctor a
patient was talking trash."

"You're kidding me?"

"Nope. The doctor came out again
&—a little more forcefully—reiterated
her original speech."

"Unbelievable."

"Yeah, it was horrible.
We're not going back.
But I did steal
a stethoscope."

the good samaritan & god's agents.

Part 1.

Mr. P., my Special-Ed prof, kept his black *Law & Order* trench coat on during class, rubbed his well-trimmed 17-day gray beard & told us a remarkable story: "The other day on Interstate 90, I passed a stalled out car along the berm. I was running late for school, but I decided to stop. So I pulled ahead of them, about a half-a-mile, & backed up. There were two women sitting inside the car, a mother & a daughter w/ a couple kids. I asked them if they were all right & they told me they were. They had a flat tire, but they had already called a tow truck. They told me it was coming. I volunteered to fix it anyway, so they wouldn't have to be stranded—especially next to the freeway. They said it was ok. I suggested that the kids wait away from the car, up on the hill. They agreed. So the kids went on the hill, & I asked them two more times if they were sure. It would only take a couple minutes. They said they were fine, but thanked me anyway. Then there was a cop car that pulled up right behind them. The strange thing was I couldn't see any city name listed on the side of the patrol car. And when the officer approached me, he said in a real serious voice, 'You can go now. You need to leave.' As I was leaving, I saw the tow truck arrive. But what upset me the most was that this cop was following me & not staying with that family."

There were about 25 students in the class, only a handful of us were really paying attention. I was. Mr. P. continued: "Well, I saw on the news that night that they were killed. Apparently, a speeding car had crossed into the berm & run into them. The mother & daughter both died in the car. The kids were still up on the hill, where I'd recommended they stay. If they were in the car, they would've died too. The news reported the accident happened at 11:35 am. I left at 11:32 am; I remember because I looked at my watch. I was late for work. So I just missed the accident. I wanted to find out their names & if the tow truck guy was all right. So I called the police station & they were expecting my call. Apparently, someone had given a description of my car leaving the scene. I asked if it was the police officer & they told me there wasn't a patrolman at the scene.

'It would've been a Cleveland cop, right?' I asked her. And she said there wasn't a report of any police officers stopping. This was weird. I asked her if I could have the tow truck driver's name & number. She said if it was anyone else, she wouldn't do it. So I called him & asked him if he had seen the cop. He told me he had seen me pull away, but there wasn't a cop, and he barely jumped out of the way of the car in time. It was just me who saw that cop. So I think he was an angel. He was so intent that I leave. I don't know why they died. Maybe I survived— because had I been changing their tire, I certainly would've died—because I still have work to do. I don't know. But I met an angel."

Part 2.

We were very drunk. I admit that now. We started drinking around 10 am, went golfing (barely) then drove to Rock Creek for my step-aunt's wedding. She was getting married at Thousand Trails Park. My grandfather, her adopted dad, is a member there. We stayed long enough for two free beers then sped away sloppily down the dirt road. I was jerking the wheel back & forth, just fucking around like an idiot & I lost control. We went rolling into a ditch. I opened my eyes once, upside down, & felt this was it. We landed right side up about 40-50 yards from where the tire tracks stopped. I think we rolled around 5 or 6 times—maybe more than that. Bill had gotten hit in the head by some floating golf clubs. In retrospect, he probably had a concussion. Plus, his leg was bleeding. The door windows were broken. We looked around & saw the stream of relatives driving by staring at us. Nobody stopped to help. They just gawked. Well, somebody had called the Sheriff because he pulled up while we were trying to shove the car out of the ditch. We nearly got it out, too.

The Sheriff wanted to know what happened. It was strange that a car should suddenly weave off the road & roll several times in the middle of a sunny day. Well, I told him, I swerved to miss a rabbit, a dog, no, it was a deer, no, it was... I just kept going up the animal kingdom. The Sheriff gave me 4 DUI tests. I walked the line just fine; I followed the pen without pause; I counted backwards from 30 to 1 in one one-thousands; I held one leg up & recited the alphabet. My breath smelled fine from the puffs of my asthma sprayer I'd taken just before we saw him, so I passed. But I did get cited for reckless driving & got my license suspended for 60 days.

When the tow truck driver picked us up, we climbed in carrying one brown bag with us. The bag broke on his floor & full beer bottles clanged each other.

Part 3.
I made an attempt to sober up after that. I kept thinking about all the what-ifs that might have happened during the accident: I was wearing a safari hat from golfing & that saved my head from getting busted up in the windshield. The hat was broken in the front where it hit the windshield. There were no other cars around at that time. There were tons of cars immediately after, but none when it happened. There weren't any telephone poles on that stretch of the road. There was no water in the ditch. Bill saw me floating around in the car while we were rolling & held me tightly against him. All these things led me to believe Somebody was watching over us poor souls. People have died from far less serious accidents.

For months I kept seeing this billboard of a little Mexican girl. I think her name was Maria Lopez, something like that. She had been killed by a drunk driver. She was only 5 years old.

nearly the partridge festival.

My hometown's annual shindig festivities
were in full boxstep when
my wife & good friend went
into the newly implanted coffee shop.

This left me alone on a
street corner—where in another setting,
at another time, a bearded woman
left to fend for her whiskers;
to sell sexual curiosities after
the circus skipped town
w/out her.

So I got a clean View-Master slide
of all the folks I used
to share detentions &
dissections with.

And their kids, too.

Citizens like the
morlocked blades of grass
beneath a tarpaulin;
citizens trudging by like a
Jack Kirby comic-book
drawing.

Later, I'm reminded of
True Temper's oily marriage
with Lake Erie, before
she met EPA.

That makes sense.

You know the hot dog girl,
every city has a version—

ugly, lonely teenage gal
w/ a half-frozen wiener.

Then there's the doctor's visit.
And the doctor is the prom queen's
ol man & the rest is
wildfire.

It had to've been tough for her.
But now she has a couple kids,
which means somebody loves her.

Or did love her.

sunday afternoon.

In a voice very distant from
Anne Sexton being suffocated
w/ a bean bag, my grandmother said—
when the sun was no longer
poking us in the eyes—
"That's the Cuyahoga County gorge.
Though it's more of a valley, really."

Mid-afternoon, Sunday, &
we're en route to visit her brother,
my great uncle, who's dying
in the hospital.

"Over there, they've got some
polo fields. For the rich kids
at a private school.
One of Cleveland's best."

"Oh, yeah?"

She'd thanked me when
I told her, a couple weeks back,
that her example has
caused me to further dislike
the squalid yardbirds that are
so commonplace
among those over 65.

"And back there, behind
the woods, is where they keep
the thoroughbred horses.
So the boys can fuck them."

"…Yeah, cause if you're not raised on a farm,
ya gotta learn 'bout it someplace else."

"You got it."

love is an attainable myth.
for Tom

I've known you for 5+ years
& have never seen you angry
or pissed off.

Well, there's always been
the WWF's Heartbreak Kid's "suck-it"
sign to rude strangers & smart-ass
comments to stray bartenders
& cranky waitresses, but never
true hostility.

That says a lot.

Especially in matters
of love.

I know you've recently
had a bad spell of
online dating encounters.

The latest one—an ambiguous voice
broadcasting choir-expulsion over
the answering machine—ended up
being a transgendered anomaly.

The penis is still there, you told me.
But it's shoved inside her, er, him.

Countless blurs of women:
a photograph, ten years old—
one from the 4th grade—
an ultrasound—

It's a *Ripley's Believe it or Not!*
exhibit of Big Foot,

the Loch Ness monster,
a griffin, lesbian vampires
makin' out w/ Medusa
tonight on *Coast to Coast*
AM radio.

These are the women
who take creative writing courses
to mince & dice the "average build"
category; these women are
there for a reason.

You've traveled to Toledo to meet
a pile of night clothes assembled
into human form; you met a forgotten
prototype Raggedy Ann doll that immediately
starts chirpin' about
anal sex & gang bangs when you pull
her string; you chatted
w/ a rock climber; you met
a missing link for dinner & wondered
how she could've Photoshopped all those
chins; you met a nice teacher & had
a good date (your best date) then found out
2 wks later she had hot-pants
for many men.

And you did meet Nicki.

You guys had a go at it &
it just didn't work.

But you remained friends.

We've all
been through it—

you're just gettin'
the condensed version.

That's a bit tougher.

See, I believe *The Creature from The Black Lagoon*
is a love story:

You've got this Olympic-swimmin'
underwater iguana whose been
chewin' on seaweed & watchin'
generations of fish have babies
& then seein' their kids have kids,
that was the Creature's life.

Until some curious humans came
explorin' & they brought Julie Adams
w/ 'em.

And she must've been on the rag
or something 'cause the Creature
goes apeshit & boards (& keeps
boardin') the ship & eventually
kidnaps Julie. Then the men—
those handsome toughies—save her
& spear-gun the Monster.
Love's like that.
It's misunderstood.

Catch a whiff of what you want
& go after it.

Don't let any damn square-jaws
stop you.

the goring of an innocent.

Jesus was beaten into meatloaf
for our sins.
That much is clear.
But at least there was
a reason for it.

While at the rodeo, an imported
hillbilly sanctuary w/the city outside
sliding grimy fingers toward
its legs, an island of national park
awkwardness, we saw a
young, Bruce Springsteen, bull riding
local get slinkied-off a
2-ton steer—then get subsequently
jitterbugged upon.

The announcer, some higher primate
form of radio DJ, said, in the voice
his 1st wife fell in love with:
"He's alright, ladies & gentlemen.
He's okay, Tony Lama.
Tony Lama, God bless the states."

Tony Lama—as I found out later,
after watching the poor booger
being stretchered out of the arena,
an assisting wrangler puppeteering
the wounded man's arm into a salute,
the same warm-blanket consolations of
parents to kids about dead pets—was
not the person before
the Dalai Lama in the hereditary lunch line.
He was just some average Texan
who made sturdy boots.

a violent year, 2007.

It's mid-October & the current
murder count in Cleveland
is 103.

The most recent additions
are 2 little girls drowned
in a bath tub by
their depressed mother.

A few others that stick out—
like poison tipped Amazon arrows
in my memory—are:
a young cop shot down the road;
a fireman that flipped out
& killed 3 of his neighbors
on the 4th of July;
a middle aged mom that was
killed by some teenagers speeding
away from the cops downtown;
& tons of kids.
Little kids.

These deaths stay in
the news spotlight for a
couple days & then they're
replaced by the next murder.

It's a rotten & terrible
assembly line.

Whatever happened to the
good ol' days when people
would get angry—geyser-exploding
angry—& would, say, like my
Uncle Bob in the early 1950s, under
a scorching, red-omelet,

late summer sun, shove
his fist, w/out thought, into
a threshing machine to
yank out stuck stalks
of wheat.

He didn't turn off the machine
& the blades were waiting for
the fingers of his left hand.

Each time, after the accident,
when Bob would feel a stream
of anger swelling in him, he'd
simply look down at that mangled
hand, covered w/ a gray sock, &
he'd quickly calm down.

crying psychosis wolf.

"Clickety-click, click...I can hear your brain working from here."
Bogart in Desperate Hours.

Among the most recent mental protests
that have sent my Aunt Lynn's brain into an
ant farm of flood preparations, is her grown
daughter moving back home.
It's an abandoned home. A shell.
Lynn lives 20 minutes away
w/ her husband, his dying mother—
permanently curdled in a queen size bed
w/ the soaps always blastin'—
& a nursemaid that may have a
boxfull of condoms decomposing
narcotics into her stomach.
The vacant house isn't even Lynn's,
it's her mother's,
who has paid for it 3 times while
Lynn's career as a nurse slowly
deteriorated from drugs & booze—
a roller coaster w/ loose nuts & bolts,
an asteroid in the atmosphere.
Lynn's clothes are still in the house, though.
That's her worry.
Mounds of clothes forming into
cliff-gradations—*Here you can see*
the Polyester Era, & below that is the
Denim Era.
Racks of clothes pressed so subway-
panic-stricken tightly, so Chinese restaurant-
aquarium close, that you can see pantsuits smeared
against the windows waiting
for a reason to break out.
It's almost menacing—like barracudas
in the kids' pool. That's why Lynn's
been calling various relatives, saying:

"I'm being held hostage. They're letting me make a few calls. And they feed me, but I'm still a hostage. Yes, I'm calling from home. Everyone's here. I can't escape."

we gotta sort things out.

In my dream, I was
in my grandparents' kitchen
& my grandfather was
cooking you in a
large pot.
When I asked if
you were done, he pulled out
all these lumps of
fleshy Play Doh & began
to stack them on top
of each other.

Finally, you were formed.
I copped a Dracula &
bit you
twice in the neck.

And like with the redness
behind under-cooked chicken,
I could tell you
weren't ready yet.

So he dismantled you
& put your pieces back
into the pot.

a story of redemption.
for Willie

Willie sat across from us
at the A.A. meeting.

She looked snowplowed by
life: weather-beaten, like
rock-salted concrete, but
there was a residual beauty
underneath the layers.

After a rehearsed lead
(w/ all
the right
dramatic
pauses
& all the perfect
emotional sighs)
Willie started talking to us.

I elbowed my ol man
in the side & quietly
said, "I think she's
interested in you."

They chatted for several minutes—
the negative space between them
shrinking as the voices grew
louder— then they exchanged
numbers & three months later
she moved into his place.

Willie used to be a rough & tumble
prostitute in Vegas. She & her pimp
would lure prospective men into
dingy motel rooms, then club 'em
in the heads once the lights

went out. "They probably killed
quite a few guys doin that,"
my dad said.

So Willie came
back to Ohio like a forgotten
boomerang, & shacked up w/ some
mean sonabitch that knocked her
around. She got tired of that crap
& stabbed him in the chest
one night.

She got 8 yrs in Marysville prison
for murder—
walked that chalk line for 6
& got off early for good behavior.

She & my ol man didn't last
beyond a couple years—
I remember her always being kind
to my sister, always being patient.

Willie went to college, became a
social worker & helped out
fellow drunks & addicts.

Love is everywhere if you just look—
Willie fell for an Indian in bad health
in Ashtabula. He died soon after
they met.

My dad believes Willie started
using coke again cause she died
a few months after the Indian,
from a heart attack.

a pick-up line.

The Target pharmacy line
that my grandmother was
waiting in
was long & curvaceous—
like the snake mound burial.

Still, but alive w/ growth.

The pharmacist
was a lonesome dot,
a vanishing point, an egg
stuck in a uterine wall.

The overhead lights
hummed & throbbed
to an imaginary beat,
casting everything &
everyone
in a faded, moldy,
jaundiced hue.

Behind her
was an elderly couple
counting couch-cushion-change
in open hands, their cart
a half-completed
periodic table of vitamins
& supplements.

In front of her
was a young man,
maybe mid-20s,
& my grandmother leaned forward—
a kind lean,
like the good witch
who would've fed Hansel & Gretel

tuna fish sandwiches
while listening to
their personal woes—
& said:

"You know,
the Mayan calendar
predicts that the world
will end in 2012.

And, you know,
the Mayans have never been
wrong in their predictions.

So, do you want to get
together sometime?"

american inventors.

I've heard it took Thomas Edison
1,000+ experiments before
he got the light bulb
just right.

I also heard 'bout an old man
from the tired, achy area
of Stringtown, PA that
figured out cuttin' a chicken's wing
a little unevenly would cause
the chicken to corkscrew
off the penis while
fuckin' it.

I don't know how many tries it
took him to get
that one just right.

the sad story of miss elizabeth, or the crown jewel.

You may remember her from
the mid-80s to the early 90s.
She was The Macho Man's wife.
A lovely brunette w/ shiny, mermaid-glittery,
Jean Harlow style, conservative-
flapper-girl sequined dresses &
Cleopatra-thick necklaces.

She always had this new employee
at the dog pound look—a wide-eyed
look: worried, anxious—always
watching her Macho Man: that balding,
bearded, reckless child
of seaweed & madness.

She was wrestling's Princess Di—
she had as much beauty & class
as a Carter Family song:
I'm thinking the *Wildwood Flower*,
particularly.

I was watching an old wrestling video
the other day of Macho Man (he'd
become King, somehow) w/ his new
girl—a Pat Benatar worn away by
loud amps & spilled beers—
Sensational (Queen) Sherri.

They fought Dusty "The American Dream" Rhodes—
the former cowboy patriarch of a
southern wrestling troupe, now reduced
to large polka dots—& Sapphire,
the relatable everywoman.

Miss Elizabeth came out to support
Dusty & Sapphire.

And I bet no one in the arena
was swearing or yelling at
their kids when she did.

She had that kind of
effect on people.

After her death (she died young—
popping pills, snorting dope, & doing
shots of booze w/ The Narcissist,
Lex Lugar) it seemed all
the women in wrestling
were suddenly too eager
to crawl on top of each other
& mimic Spring Break
lesbian-friendly videos.

There were less families in
the audience & more & more lonely men
crammed together—all gasping in unison
& sharing the same fantasies.

customer service.

The mother was this 50+
pawn shop clone of Martha Stewart.
The sorta woman who'd plan Avon parties
years in advance; a
swollen tofu plank w/ dyed blonde hair &
teeth like a pore strip: wormy & scattered.
She demanded to know why
I kicked her pudgy Augustus Gloop—
her Pillsbury doughboy of a son—
out of the store.

"Well, we got this policy,"
& I pointed at the
big sign on the door,
"no kids under 18 without
a parent."

"He's got plenty of money &
he's not going to make a mess!"

"You're missing the point," I said.
"What if all the black kids
I kick out every day saw
one white kid in here
without a parent.
It's unfair."

"I can't believe you just said that.
That's racist & you're discriminating
against kids," she scowled,
like a sour President Johnson
during Reconstruction.

It wasn't a soapbox derby,
it was simply a soap box.
She needed an issue &
I was it.

"Look, lady. I just follow the store rules.
This isn't my place. I just work here.
That's it."

The Dalai Lama's cantankerous landlady
finally decided to stay since
she couldn't debate the point
to my absent boss.

The cannibal's-buffet delight spent
65 bucks on Chinese plastic crap that
Augustus would open, diddle
for a moment, then
toss out.

She left the store like an
80s sitcom cliffhanger—
all huffy w/ promises
to return.

The very next day she returned
& continued in on me as if
I was the reason
dodos were extinct.

It was the same script.
Yesterday was the rehearsal dinner,
today was the wedding.

The one fat difference this time
was her credit card # wouldn't
work, so I went in the back room &
fondled the fax machines.
When I came back out,
she was gone.

She'd taken the Jolly Green Giant's son,
more junk, her card, & simply
vanished.
Well, maybe not simply.
She vanished with much effort.

We pulled some *Matlock* tricks &
deciphered her cuneiform signature
from the previous day's credit card slip
& discovered she was a judge.

She was the district's judge
& she was up for re-election.

Which she didn't get.

pillow talk.

We didn't quite agree that
if aliens came to meet
us earthlings the 1st thing
we'd do is try
to fuck 'em.

Like puppies humpin' legs.

In a week these
(& I'm just guessin' here)
2-ft tall half-cod/
half-zucchini-bread concoctions
would be on a website
with us humans licking
their assholes:
www.welcumthealiens.com

She tells me I'm probably
the only one—
well, maybe there are three others—
that would think that.

Yeah, I know. That's why they
haven't stopped by for a visit.

She rolls over & sets
the alarm for 9 am.

warehouse duties.

The Amazing Gary,
a Houdini-hopeful
that's now settled
for simple magic tricks that
make the kids smirk
& the parents groan,
has been working w/ me
in the store's warehouse.
The warehouse should be
featured on a city tour of
unsafe working environments:
you got the miner's cave uptown,
with real charbroiled lungs
on display & dead canary key chains
in the gift store.
Witness the maimed & mutilated
children in early
industrial factories.
Get your picture with Tiny—
he's only a head, but he can
still pull levers
with his mouth.
Then there's us—
not nearly as susceptible
to injury & disfigurement,
but still entertaining.
Behold, as lead paint chips
fall like snow from the ceiling,
you can hear—if you listen real close—
a rabid raccoon eating
Sugar Daddys, the last flappings
of trapped robins, the busy
traffic of cockroaches, and
that melodic swish is the workers
tossing their urine out the windows,
a la Middle Ages.

So it's in this environment,
usually in the before & after,
that Gary was telling me about
one of the hood friends
he used to run with:
"There was this bigwig used car salesman
on the Eastside that wanted
some fast insurance money, so he
recruited Sal & me to 'steal' his new Buick.
'Do a number on it,' he says.
So we snag the car & drive it /smash it /
pound it / into whatever walls & railings
we can find.
For the icing, we shot three dozen bullets into it &
poured gasoline all over it &
watched it go up like the 4th of July.
We got paid well & Sal
was happy.
After that, I did some telemarketing.
Selling gold & silver to saps.
Sal ended up having a
heart attack one day
at home.
You see, he was pretty fat.
It just got worse after
I knew him.
Plus, he just drank beer all day
& stuffed his face with junk food.
So he died in a Lazy Boy,
unable to get outta
the chair.
When they found his body,
like, four days later, his cat
had eaten his face off.

I guess it was hungry."

outside the door.

Part 1.
Sarah came back into
Tom's life after 2 months
of silence—a long
commercial break.

Tom was doing alright
w/out her.
He had gotten her
outta his system.

Then she drops a letter
on his doorstep—like a
shot down stork lugging
a fat baby—& she
expects something.

I don't know what.

Part 2.
There are tons of
lightning bugs
in our back yard tonight.
They're all over the trees
& bushes—Christmas lights
tossed like wedding rice.

I'm glad to see them.
I heard pollution was
killing them off.

Not tonight, though.

I call my wife, Trin, to come
& take a look & she tells
me a little about them—

"There are different species
of lightning bugs that
use distinctive blinking
patterns," she says.

"The males are the ones
flying around looking for
their matching pattern.
When they find a compatible
female, they get busy.

Then that female changes
her blinking pattern, to lure
a different male in, &
then she eats him."

It no longer seems
so peaceful
after I hear that.

government check.

Hillbilly Mike—no relation to
the wrestler Hillbilly Jim (they're
just linked through nicknames &
unmanageable beards) came
to Northeast Ohio like a
burp of coal dust from
deep West Virginia.

It's said he brought
his wife—a mythical creature,
a shoplifted Yeti, that none
have seen.

In addition to getting a
government check for providing
a very strange home
to nearly half a dozen
foster kids in a trailer park
spitting distance from
Lake Erie, Mike delivered
pizza for a restaurant
I cooked at.

He'd moan & give the
delivery customers a quick, sad
A&E bio about his financial woes
& why he
deserved more
than a 3 dollar tip.

A few people complained &
Mike was fired.

It was around this time
I paid him to change
my brake pads.

He worked on my truck in
my grandfather's orchard,
w/ all the dead & cut down
apple trees, like amputated limbs,
surrounding him.

He kept working during a
thunderstorm that came
in buckets.

I didn't have the heart
to tell him to stop.

options & stagnancy.

The living room surroundings were
always changing: updated couches,
different paintings, bigger TVs &
a more comfortable Lazy Boy.

The cigarette smoke was like
a dirty sweater—
thick & clotting.

It was an ongoing still life
photography experiment.
My grandmother—my maternal
grandmother—not to be confused
w/ my pleasantly weird other grandma,
or my dead step-grandmother or my
alive step-grandmother—
aged slowly over the
past 30+ years.
But she always remained in
the center chair, w/ remote control
& television warmly close.

Occasionally, a few of the relatives
would go to Biloxi, Vegas, etc.

There were birthdays to remember,
holidays to celebrate, meals to cook.

Life's busy enough, then there are
all the activities to plan for.

She mentioned to me, once, that
when she was a kid, she wanted
to be a geologist.

I never forgot that.

keep that diaphragm in, or the early days.

"She had a white blouse, a blue skirt and legs.
Wow! And legs. So I says to myself,
'I need to meet that broad.'" John Rocchio,
one half of the world's oldest married couple.

for Trinity.

Part 1.

Sometimes you might pray for someone
to come along & help you, to fill that
large hole in yourself, & maybe
this is a prayer said in
great desperation—
almost without hope of fulfillment.
Maybe those prayers are the most honest,
'cause they are desperate &
'cause you came along:

a little tulip that escaped from
the floral shop & now is chicken-dancing,
nearly being pinballed by
the various storefront windows,
the new album ads, the sandwhich deals,
the basement book sale—
a Kewpie doll on the lam in a
pink-jacketed, fast-forward blur
past me, while I arrange
the final cigarettes in a couple
ventriloquist dolls' mouths.

Part 2.

I saw a 9/11 documentary the other night,
& something that stuck in me, like
extra-large pins in a voodoo doll, or
a myopic acupuncturist, were the
last conversations loved ones had.

For example, the male passengers on
that poor plane headin' towards the
White House.
They knew what had to be done,
so they called their wives &
said their good-byes.
Imagine those final words.
You've got two minutes to say everything,
& what'll you say? *I love you.*
I love you & I'm glad we found
each other.
You've made me very happy.

I want to treat every day I'm with you
like that last conversation.

Part 3.
I was, before you came along, a
zombie telemarketer sellin' valentine cards
to anyone who'd take 'em.
I don't regret meeting & mingling,
like shelless hermit crabs on the
edge of an ocean, with all the
women I knew before you.

I wasn't ready for you
& you weren't
prepared for me.

Our hearts needed tune-ups.

The lassoing attempts by rough-draft-
amateur-Mormon-wannabes to win us
over & convince us to accept
ideas against our hearts—

well, that junkyard behavior wears on
your soul like refrigerator mold.

But we did find each other.
& then we started to walk.

Part 4.
The walks were somethin'.
The walks are what bear-trapped
my heart—if I were a bowerbird,
I would've just started to take
rumba lessons & begun to
litter my place with
dumpster-picked jewels.

The early courtship.

We never paid much attention to
the Fisher Price houses along those
green back streets.

I remember focusin' on the
different shrubs & bushes
that stretched beyond
the fences & gates—like prisoners
with their arms between bars—
& the puddles on the sidewalk
with dead earthworms (the victims
of a disastrous family vacation) &
the words we paddle-balled
back & forth.

Thoreau mentioned the
magnified importance of words
while chattin' with his pal
across Walden Pond.

I say there is a tighter intimacy, like
the blood vessels shared by
Siamese twins, when two people are
walkin' & just allowin' thoughts
to come & go—
no encodin' & decodin'—
no complications or translations—
just the honest talk of two people
gettin' to know each other.

And the smells. I remember the smells.
Wet smells of Spring being squeezed through
a strainer & you get all the flowers, soil, birds,
grass, alive-ness of everything.
Like a garden; my grandfather's garden
the morning after a rainfall.

The bean sprouts of love.

a late eulogy, or a belief in signs.
for Mary

Part 1.
My wife & I were nearly run over
by the 1st place, blue ribbon winning
horse drawn caisson at the
Geauga County Fair.
Amidst all the glittering silver & turquoise
stirrups & reins, we heard
a gangly, stringbean teen shouting
foghorn warnings at us to move.
I suppose they're tough to brake
once they get momentum—
like a runaway idea or
a chariot's desire for more.
Still, if this was 6 yrs back,
I'd have punched the kid out.

But now I'm reformed.

Part 2.
President Lincoln's body was escorted
by a funeral caisson, once off the
long train ride—
it seems many presidents were.

There's something more personal
about the slower pace of the horses,
something that gives bystanders
more time for personal reflection.
It's almost like the horses are
yanking everyone's stray, beloved
memories of the deceased out of their
minds & into the open air.

My Great Aunt Mary's funeral
had a caisson.

She communicated her desire
for one a few nights after
her death, when
she called her daughter collect,
as the dead & spirits usually do:
through dreams.
Our personalized Pony Express
mailbox. Cheaper than
passenger pigeons & crammed
full of raw emotion.
It happens like that sometimes.
Remember: the angel Gabriel told Joseph
to get Mary & baby Jesus the heck outta town.
The Bible's stuffed w/ visitors
in dreams.

Aunt Mary's daughter believed
the dream & told her brother, Gary,
about it the next day.
Gary pulled a lot of strings & favors
to find a caisson on such short notice.
Of course he found one.
It was meant to be.

Part 3.
I just heard a radio program about
a Native American teacher & storyteller
named Esther "Blue Water" Martinez.
She died last weekend from a drunk driver.
At her funeral, the whole community
had witnessed a draught-breaking, sprinkler-like
rainstorm while the sun still showed
its bloodshot Cyclops eye.
The Pueblos interpreted it as a sign
that Blue Water had reached
her destination.

At Mary's funeral, I'm told,
there was a lone horse
that had escaped from a nearby ranch
& stood, ardent crossing guard,
on the road in front of
the cemetery.
That stray horse, as dutiful hall monitor,
wouldn't allow anyone to pass.
You never saw this on *Rifleman*
or *Bonanza.*
The viewing audience wouldn't buy it,
but here it happened.
And when the horse drawn caisson
appeared, w/ Clydesdales as large
& beautiful as Pegasus, there were
all of her grandkids following behind—
like a loving movement, hands
touching hands & warm, peaceful waves
bringing comfort & peace.

Someone recognized that solitary horse
& escorted it home & someone else
saw the horse hoofprints wreathed
around Mary's tombstone.
And everyone remembered this
Sunday School teacher—
this mother, this wife, this
grandmother, this aunt, this
child of God, this
Senator for the Lord—
as an honest-to-goodness,
wonderful human being.

You can't ask for much
more than that.

the honeymoon.

We were on the Gulf Coast
2 months before Katrina
started her Biblical, Royal Rumble,
storm tour through
the region— stopping
to sign autographs in
Biloxi, MS.

I remember driving on I-10
all along the coastline—
Picasso's Blue Period skies & a
fresh blue Kool Aid ocean.
We passed the Veterans' Home
many times—
it was between Jefferson Davis' pad
& the George E. Ohr (mad-potter)
museum, both tourist hot-spots.

Paul served in WW2 & Korea.
He was in the Navy.
We met him 6 months after
Katrina, at my Dad's place in
Geneva, OH.

He told us about the ocean water slowly
coming into the Veterans' Home like
a broken pipe in
the basement.
Then it really came in—
like a water park disaster.
The water lifted furniture,
vending machines, people...

Paul yelled for everyone to head
for higher ground, so they all
went to the 2nd & 3rd floors.

The water followed them like
a B-movie monster up the
stairs & stopped.

They stayed there on the
upper floors—for hours or days,
Paul didn't specify—his focus
now on leaving
his home:
"They took us out by boat &
I was one of the last to leave.
I saw the water carrying our
home's sign away.

That was too much for me.
That was the worst part for me."

The last I heard of Paul
was he moved into his son's
house in Georgia.

Paul lived on the third floor
in an almost widow's peak.
His grandkids' loud music traveled
through the vents, up the stairs, like fog,
& interrupted Paul while he thought
of his old home, his friends, &
while he wrote his son—his landlord—
the $400 monthly rent check.

sports bars.

It wasn't too long ago
that beer gardens had just
one lonesome black & white TV
nested high on top of a
rickety beer cooler, usually
showing the day's news reports
in a snowstorm of static—
& the bar patrons' loneliness,
that dripped from them
like percolated coffee, couldn't
be camouflaged by the
subtle moans from
the insignificant jukebox.

Nowadays, the style
is sports bars.
I had to go into such
a joint, after church, to get
a refund for "concert tickets"
from the previous night.
Since *No Child Left Behind*, it seems
everyone has fuzzy math skills—
including this bar owner who
overbooked the midget rock show
& received a personalized
telegram from
the Fire Marshall.

Very early Sunday afternoon,
the bar was flooded w/ thick, sweaty
meatheads—the older guys all
lamenting stories relatable to
Springsteen's *Glory Days* & the
younger fellas listening, attentively,
while drinking shots in
boring apprenticeship.

Everyone stared neck-craned at
the rows & rows of supersized TVs,
all blaring dozens of sports games—
from pee-wee football to
celebrity frog hunting—& snuggled
into the commercial breaks were
half a dozen strippers protoplasming
around the nucleus of the bar,
handing out their cards &
giving small squeezes
on the arms,
on the thighs,
of the men.

The TVs' sports announcers' voices
all pureed together & the
blurriness of the voices
itching for something & the
foghorn warnings from the 7,000+ song
jukebox were all making
me dizzy.
The words of John the Baptist,
"A brood of vipers," lay on
the edge of my brain—

a welcome interruption,
a realization behind the curtains,
a reason not to come back.

abusive relationships.

Amazing Gary used his telemarketing skills
to badmouth the restaurant's resident pianist.
"Tell me," he'd say, w/ all sorts
of roller-coastering muscle twitches & head bobs,
"does anybody tango or waltz or
feel entertained when ol Jim Lake
is playin' piano?"

The thick Italian restaurant owner—
who may or may not have been
Bruno Sammartino's uncle—said
"No. No one a'dances. No one a'twists."

"Well, there you go. I'll entertain 'em."

So Amazing Gary showed up on a
Friday night w/ hidden fishing line in
his sleeves, coin tricks in his pockets,
fake thumbs w/ pulsing red lights &
he swaggered table to table, pushing his
magic act & kicking dirt on
Jim Lake's entertaining corpse
whenever he could.

Some relationships begin like that—
ruining the previous guy's rep.

My wife's friend Tina hooked up
w/ an old flame after the divorce,
& every chance he got
he'd remind her
of her ex-husband's infidelities:
"I'll never cheat on ya, sugar.
Bob's a sonabitch! He's got it coming!
He'll get it from me one of these days
for cheating on you!"

Of course, the new man, Dan, was a meth-head,
had maxed-out Tina's credit cards, & had
hit three cars on the freeway while
driving drunk.

I told Amazing Gary—after he said they
hadn't put his name in the paper yet, but
still had Jim Lake's name listed—
"Keep referencing the points that
no one danced after eating their spaghetti dinners
when Jim was there, and keep reminding them
about the mistake in the newspaper.

Oh, yeah—I'd watch myself in the
parking lot afterwards.
You never know about these
piano players & their itchy fingers."

the irregulars.

We've been gettin' picky
w/ our karaoke bars—
we simply want a place
w/ a big song book &
democratic rotation.
No favorites.
Once a DJ shows vulnerability
to bribes—a pretty *Hee Haw*
chick says 'nice hair' or some
Dale Earnhardt fan brings a
free beer—it becomes
a tyranny &
it's time to move along.

We're karaoke gypsies in Cleveland.
We've had our mics cut off
at Woo-Long—a Chinese restaurant
downtown where the cooks
regularly drop live eels
on the floor.
We've been heckled (& have heckled)
at The Missing Link, as the crowd
slid towards the ultra-lonely
& the physically deformed—
like a backup circus tent.
We've had beer thrown at us,
along w/ curses, at
The Secret Box.
We've been intentionally ignored &
our song slips became
Amelia Earhart love letters
in Willoughby.

But the other night at The Lost Island,
we met the resident karaoke alpha-male
& he actually thanked us for coming out.

I told him he does some
mean Led Zeppelin.

So we'll see how it goes:
there are already established
irregulars here—

Snickers, a white Ella Fitzgerald
w/ the voice to make it big, but
the candy-plump body to be ridiculed
by celeb mags if she did.

Guido fulfills the expectation
for a Meat Loaf song—he seems
kind & probably secretly
loves one of the bartenders.

Then there's Klaus: a ruddy, Ole Anderson
of a German who's been avoiding
sauerkraut & kielbasa so he can
catch that inner chi for some
Al Green.

This just might be our
Emerald City, our
Island of Lost Toys,
our new home.

floating parents.

He was my mother-in-law's shack-up job
after the divorce.
Apparently, Hal was the Casanova
of free hot dogs & popcorn
at K-Mart cafeterias & had
a small speed boat.

Things didn't work out.
It's always a strain being
a replacement parent.
Like worn out shingles or
a loose floorboard.

So life continued.
My mother-in-law found Jesus,
& Hal found his brother bed-ridden
w/ depression:
drinking a 12-pack a day & digging
holes into his leg, spots
loosened by psoriasis, until
he reached the bone.

an immigrant's journey.

Fred's relationship w/cops seems bi-polar, at best.
He was on his own at the age of 10, helping
Pakistani cops sell the drugs they
confiscated from dealers.
As a young man, he'd beat up these
same cops: "They didn't have guns over there.
So if a cop fucks with you, you just slap
him around."
After traveling through several continents
& eating almost any mammal or reptile that came
within 5 miles of him, he was in Chicago—
home of Sandburg & Brooks,
the last vestige of honest music.
Fred married an Italian woman & soon
after she started fooling around with her
former boyfriend.
Fred caught them together in his bed,
but he was cool.
He became uncool after the divorce,
while the ex & her new/old beau had Fred's
daughter for a weekend:
"The boyfriend spanked my daughter, man.
She told me. You don't touch my girl.
So I was drunk & drove over there.
They had a restraining order on me. But I didn't care.
I busted in there, pulled that guy into the yard & beat
the shit outta him. They called the cops, but the cop
that came was my friend. He said,
'Fred, what're you doing? They got a restraining order.'
I said, 'Man, he slapped my kid.'
That was that.
My friend locked that guy up for a night.
And the next day he moved
to Louisiana.
I went after him, &
then he moved to Texas."

a matter of pride.

This isn't my car.
It's a rental—
my truck was rear-ended
& the lady that hit me
is coughin' up dough for
this love seat of a vehicle.

They were going to give me
a car "with stains on the seats"
like a prison mattress
or a frat-house couch
but instead I got this
$20,000+ Nissan & as
I sit & wait for the windows
to defrost, I notice the
same elderly Russian couple
from the other night.

Their small bodies, patch-quilted
coats & slight hunch backs
are like broken Christmas lights
in this winter storm.

They treat every parking meter
like a crime scene—
looking meticulously for
any money.

My wife had tried to give
the old lady some change
& she refused it.

"They're not bums," I told her
the next day, as we walked past
some old, & I mean old, buzzard
puffin' an arthritic pipe w/ fat,

cartoon puffs of smoke,
& haulin' a nicotine-yellow
kitchen sink on
his bicycle.

"There's a caste system with bums
& the desperate poor.
That couple is working.
You should leave some change
by the meter, if you
want to help."

We turned around to see if
that antique fella wrecked
his bike on the icy road—

his tire tracks were already
covered by the snow.

the birds & bees do it.

The sun's dropping like a sluggish yo-yo
& I'm stuck between two
fast moving trains—
if this were a public shower, I'd
feel uncomfortable. But it isn't
& there is a fine breeze coming
from the trains, Tom Waits is
singing cement about lost love,
& the day feels like a bruised plum—
cool & squishy.
It's one of those moments
where you feel absolute serenity
& peace & if these trains were
to de-rail & flatten me into
a cheap pancake, it'd be alright.

I'd just want you here
w/ me.

internet porn.

We had heard floatin' rumors that
Thailand had elephants doin' their
own Abstract paintings.

So we went a-Googlin' for these
2-ton Jackson Pollocks, & what
we learned was: yes, at one time,
elephants were given brushes & paints &
canvases & told to "paint their
feelings."

And they did.

They painted their depression
at being separated from their families,
from their homes.

They expressed freedom
in brilliant colors
& emotional swirls.

This soon became a tourist slot machine.
A bill-snatcher to be used
on the passersby.

Elephants that were previously used to
haul logs to & fro were now given
French berets, long cigarettes,
& were expected to make these
poor Thai farmers
millionaires.

But the trend collapsed,
as all trends do.

The white tourists journeyed to Zaire

& bought clumsy Rodin interpretations
that gorillas were sculptin'.

So, now, on the 2nd website we've found,
the elephants are sportin' thigh-highs,
wearin' curly, blond wigs & are
vacuum-cleanin', w/ their long trunks,
hidden peanuts from
their owners' bodies.

This seems to have brought
the wayfarin' travelers back,
for now.

the machine shop.

Externally,
the machine shop was a
plain, brown box.
The building might contain illegal
dog fights or be a satellite church
for Jehovah's Witnesses.

Inside, it was a different story.

The sun was strained through
used coffee filters & the
few quivering fluorescent bulbs
were coated in a layer
of fog.

It was a cavern—& instead of
the standard prehistoric cartoons featuring
Ungh! the tribe leader pounding a
saber-toothed tiger senseless—you had
sausage-linked *Gilligan's Island* sex scenes
freshly peeled from *Hustler* or
Penthouse mags superglued
throughout the work area.

My job that summer was an ongoing
circus-contortion of metal: bending it,
twisting it, cutting it, spot-welding it…
My co-workers were a subterranean lot:
trolls, orcs, Bosch cave drawings,
half-finished hieroglyphs w/ ever-present
cigarettes in mouths constantly
stampeding through the brownish, hardened,
oatmeally grime that lay barnacled

everywhere—on them, on the machines,
on the tools, on the time clock—
like a Titanic exhibit.
And, as if for adornment, like parsley
or basil leaves, every few inches there
were curled, metal shavings jutting out
of the grime, like pubic hairs
in a bar of soap.

The Adam of this new grime paradise—
the foreman, the boss, the leader
of the pack—looked like every
white guy that's been drunk & tasered
on *COPS*: large forehead, facial hair
that never really sprouted, sleeves
rolled up & a smirk hacked from an
alligator that just got fed.
And all the guys there had one
desperate ambition—
to get the foreman's job.
Those 2 or 3 bucks more an hour
would go a long way, they figured.

And maybe that's why he told me
this story—boss's privilege:
"Ya, ah took this broad into da office
after-hours, & was fuckin her on mah desk.
It was all dark, & all ah can hear is her kid,
four er five, tryin ta git into da office.
Da kid's ballin, & Ah'm tellin da dame
ta shuddup, & tellin her ta stay put
& shuddup, cuz she wants
ta see da brat.

And ah finish, & keep her
there listenin ta dat brat
cry outside da door."

hudson & a taste of violence.

Mobile, Alabama had a bunch
of shipping ports once.
Maybe it still does.
Hudson was working near the
docks one afternoon in '63, when he
& his pal saw: "some foreigner with
a real bad limp. Just kinda hoppin' along.
So my friend says, *'straighten-up, mothafucka!'*
He was just kiddin' the guy,
but the dude comes over to us
& slaps me in the side of the face
cause Ah was laughin'.
And Ah says, *'Man, you've done it!'*
Ah went & got a brick, busted it
in half & started ta beat that fucka
in the head with it."

"Jesus, did you kill the guy?"

"Nah. Mah friends pulled me off
before Ah could."

it was a survivor's tale.

It could be a new Greek myth:
Zeus—upset & rampaging like
a mad bull in the prize-winning
tulip garden— hurls
w/ bowling champion accuracy
8 lightning bolts
8 seperate times at
George, the modest & humble
park ranger.

We'll never know what he
did to Zeus, but we do know
that each lightning bolt took
something from George:
the 1st one took his left big toe in '42;
the 2nd one seared his eyebrows off;
the 3rd one gave him cramps
in a shoulder;
the 4th & 5th messed up his
equilibrium;
the 6th gave him burns all
up & down his arms;
the 7th ruined his sideburns;
& the 8th bolt was in
the form of a beautiful woman
that broke poor George's heart.

So much that he couldn't recover &
he killed himself a few
weeks later.

you never know who you'll find.

Linesville, PA didn't have a mess
of riff raff cartoon stick people loitering
on street corners.
Nope.
Linesville, like its
Thanksgiving dinner table neighbors,
is a quiet, warm-blankets-from-the-dryer
feeling town surrounded by full acres
of woods & tall corn fields.

My wife & I almost moseyed, but then decided
to walk, into Jamestown—a town pumpkin-hurling
distance from Linesville—& spotted
a couple lonely signs plugging
a *Woodcarver's Gallery*.

The elderly leprechaun that owned
this gallery—which wasn't filled w/
chainsawed totem poles or intricately hacked
canoes like I'd originally thought, but rather
w/ beautifully carved portraits of ducks, geese,
lighthouses, dams, Popes, & more—
was like Van Gogh had he been
a woodcarver.
The curator & sculptor was a gentle
Dutchman named John Vanhedden or something
like that. A curious kind gnome that actually did
own a pair of wooden shoes, did make windmills,
did like to squeeze your shoulders & flick
your nose as he told you numerous stories of
farming, coming to the states w/ ten bucks in
his pockets, the death of his father at 96, his
wife's recent hospital stay, his 10 brothers & 1 sister,
& this story:
"When the Nazis invaded Holland,
we didn't put up much resistance, you know.

We couldn't fight the German Army.
So after a small skirmish, the Nazis lodged
in our barn. They stayed a couple nights until
the Allies came—Canadians, British, Americans—
then the Allies lodged in our barn.
Eisenhower was just a couple miles away,
you know. So I was a young man, 15, 16, &
I wanted to see the American General. So I rode
my bike toward the battles & then a Nazi solider
called me over to a bush & said, 'Get down.
There's a battle going on.'
So I stayed in the bush & right then tanks
started driving by, & then the bullets.
So that Nazi saved my life.
Later on, our barn was destroyed by bombs.
All the village barns were.
We had a fireproof basement in the house
so we stayed there.
When the bombing stopped, my father
opened the basement door & looked out.
A Nazi tried shooting him.
The bullet went through his pants leg,
you know. And my father says,
'Hey, I'm not a solider! You almost shot me!'
And the solider says, 'I'm sorry.'
Later on, that same Nazi wanted to stay with us,
& my father says ok.
So the Nazi stripped off his uniform & was ready
to come over but changed his mind.
Then the Allies' tanks came in, you know.
And my father went over to them & says,
'There's a Nazi hiding in that ditch over there.'
The Allies went & grabbed that Nazi,
you know. They took him away.

Now you two are in love, right?
Listen here…"

love is an elusive fishing lure.
for Tom

My dream: in the shallow end of the stream,
bodies were squeezed around turbines.
The turbines were under water & resembled
large communion wafers, half-dollars,
something circular—
a saw, perhaps.
Trin & I found ourselves
floating on a rotten 2x4 &
when we reached the shore,
a couple alligators—4 to 6 feet each—
came after us.
The 2x4, which I was going
to hit the gators with, sank quickly
into the deep, deep stream—
Loch Ness Monster deep,
new species of mean
fluorescent fish deep.
The gators had jagged jaws
like thick hacksawed puzzle pieces.
We kept backing away from them
& they kept coming—
I was throwing seaweed & our clothes
at their eyes— I remembered seeing
a *National Geographic* program about this—
& just when I was getting ready to wrestle
the damn things, Trin woke me up
by clanging dishes around.

I don't tell Tom about this
dream, later that night, while we
stand there in my kitchen—
w/ its sickly green lead-painted walls
filling each spot of missing tile like a
tongue or a cigarette in the mouth;
w/ its new ant traps like strip malls that

sober worker ants enter to relax
& complain about the queen, then exit
like separated optical rods: all wobbly
& hectic...

Intead, I start a lecture tour about
his recent love interest gone awry:
"It's a meat-market mentality many
of these young women take towards dating,
nowadays. A desperate immediacy.
Drive-thru love affairs. MTV-inspired longevity.
12-items-or-less-one-night-stands. A hypnotist's
fear of commitment.
This is especially true in cities, I feel.
Take Martha, for example—
she's this old bitty, pushin' 90 by now,
who lives across the street
from my grandparents.
One time, my grandparents left me
their house key so I could check up
on the place while they went outta town.
Well, I did. But I also brought over
a Russian chick I was foolin' around with
at the time. Martha—that hoot owl, that pair
of eyes permanently stuck to the window—
she saw us & she told.
I had to give back the key.
Now, what I'm sayin' is we need Martha.
Society needs Marthas.
They're our neighborhood watches.
Yeh, despite being a pain-in-the ass
with all their gossip-weavin' & constant
judgments of others & always wearin' binoculars
around their necks like a lifeguard's whistle—
they serve an important societal purpose
in regulatin' reputations & rumors.

See, if Jane had done what she
did to you in a small town—
just took off while things were
going well & cookin'—then Martha, &
other old hags like her, would start discussin'
the issue like it was a debate
'bout the death penalty.
Jane would've changed her tune
through peer pressure—or at least
thought more carefully 'bout her actions
the next time.

But, because of the large amount
of anonymity that cities provide,
people can toss aside each other, throw away
emotions & hearts like recyclables.
It is her fault, but—on a wider
scale—she's just blendin' in.

There's no social pressure for these
people to act with courtesy towards
one another.

I know there are a couple decent
women floatin' around—
there's gotta be.

Maybe we can go to Amish country
this weekend.

Just to look around."

eulogy for the living.

We were driving to Tillamook,
a coastal city in Oregon.
To get there we had to drive
through the Neahkahnie Mountains—
a driver's-ed course sponsored
by NASCAR; a prototype salamander
climbing the evolutionary ladder
out of the primordial cafeteria slop
onto solid ground, only to get
stuck, immediately, in a
Minotaur's maze.

There was this continual swerving &
braking, pausing & pollywogging around
Alfred Hitchcock silhouetted curves—
the whole time being tailgated
by a few lonesome stragglers—
red cars that had
important business meetings
at Grandma's place.

Oregon's lucky, they've got plenty
of their old growth woods left.
And before the trees got too thick,
spread their branches like
crossing guards, & forbid all
radio transmissions to enter,
we did get to hear one
last program on NPR.

It was about a poet named Jack Gilbert.
He had just won some prestigious award
for one of his books.
He's 82 & rents a small room
from one of his friends
in Massachusetts.

Jack read a couple poems &
they were solid.
But what impressed me most
was his philosophy on life.
He kept repeating this point—
like a Jelly Roll Morton song lyric,
like a local meteorologist reporting
an Ice Age front that
avoids his city—
"It's a wonderful privilege just
to be here…just to be allowed
to be alive…the sweetness of what
we're allowed to experience…"

It is a privilege, a nice pension,
to be here on this
muddy, rubber-band-ball
floating around
in space.
It is a blessing to be here,
even if it's just for a blip
on eternity's radar.

Now that I'm thinking
about it, I'm glad to have met
you all in this life,
for all these moments—
here & now in these mountains
the Nehalen tribe called
Neahkahnie: The Resting Place
of the Supreme Being.

Very special thanks to:
my family, for all my mad and crazy genetic spaghetti;
Dave, for believing in me; Alice, for your patience and
effort; Kat and Phyllis, for early inspiration; Suzanne at
Mac's Backs, for your help and support; & all my friends
(Tom, Bess, Sam, Anthony, Justin, etc.) for coming to my
scattered readings.

Thank you Trinity, for everything.

Jason Floyd Williams was born in 1974 and lives in Cleveland, Ohio with his wife, Trinity. He has held more than 30 jobs since he was 15 years old: roofer, dishwasher, cook, delivery driver, gas station attendant—and general labor in too many factories. He received his BA in English from Cleveland State University in 2004 and currently works at a vintage toy shop.

www.interiornoisepress.com

www.ingramcontent.com/pod-product-compliance
Lightning Source LLC
Chambersburg PA
CBHW051724040426
42447CB00008B/969